# NEPAL

## THREE WEEKS
## OF
## CULTURAL AND SHAMANIC IMMERSION

## APRIL 2006

By Susan Chapman Melanson

## Acknowledgements

Lines from Bob Seger's "Kathmandu" are from Bob Seger and the Silver Bullet Band's Great Hits, Vol. 2 (Capitol, 2003).

Lines from Led Zeppelin's "Stairway To Heaven" are from Led Zeppelin IV (aka ZOSO) (Atlantic, 1971 original release).

Reference to Vince Gill's "Let There Be Peace On Earth" (Mca Special Products, 1993).

Lines from the Moody Blues' "Vintage Wine" are from "Sur la Mer" (Columbian, 1988).

Lines from Michael Buble's "Home" (Wea International, 2005).

Lines from Lee Greenwood's "God Bless the USA" from "Lee Greenwood Greatest Hits, Vol. 2" (Mca Special products, 1994).

NEPAL: THREE WEEKS OF CULTURAL AND SHAMANIC IMMERSION, APRIL 2006. Copyright 2006 by Susan Chapman Melanson. All rights reserved. Printed in the United States of America. No part of this book may be used or reproduced in any manner whatsoever without written permission except in the case of brief quotations embodied in critical articles and review. For information address Susan Chapman Melanson, 14 Husky Haven, South Hiram, ME 04041.

FIRST US EDITION

ISBN: 978-0-6151-3559-5

*Photographs: Susan Chapman Melanson, Mujiba Cabugos and Pramod Sapkota*

1. Nepal 2. Shamanism 3. Buddhism, Tibetan 4. Peters, Larry G.
5. Melanson, Susan Chapman

**TITLE PAGE:** Statue of Garuda, Durbar Square, Kathmandu, Nepal. Taken by Susan Chapman Melanson.

This book is dedicated
to my husband, Art,
without whom this story
would not have come to pass.

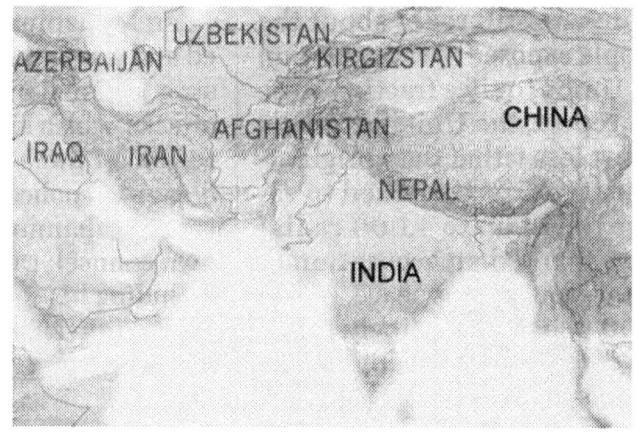

Where In The World Is Nepal?

## PREFACE

I have tried to bring the reader along on my life-changing adventure to exotic Nepal as I expand and enhance my abilities as a shamanic practitioner. The sightseeing portion of our trip was thwarted by anti-monarchy demonstrations, a nationwide strike and curfews imposed by the king to try to subdue the unrest. Nine fellow adventurers shared this chapter of my life. I have included in-depth details of my own healings and experiences in both ordinary and non-ordinary reality. We all had very personal encounters with Spirit, deities and our own reflections. As with any family, I was privy to many of these insights. I have opted, however, to record only my own details in deference to the privacy of Denise, Erica, Jeff, Larry, Mujiba, Sarah, Susan, June and Burt. Nevertheless, their experiences and healings, insights and encouragement, caring and sharing were a big part of my experience and I thank them all from the bottom of my heart for being my family for twenty-four precious days.

Namaste,
Susan Chapman Melanson
August 2006

## TABLE OF CONTENTS

| | | |
|---|---|---|
| Dedication and Map "Where In The World is Nepal?" | | 3 |
| Preface | | 5 |
| Table of Contents | | 7 |
| | | |
| Chapter 1: | Prelude to Nepal | 9 |
| Chapter 2: | Political Background | 19 |
| Chapter 3: | Gathering in Los Angeles March 28-29 | 20 |
| Chapter 4: | My Fellow Adventurers | 23 |
| Chapter 5: | March 29-30 The Final Leg of Three Days of Travel | 30 |
| Chapter 6: | March 31 Arrival in Kathmandu | 33 |
| Chapter 7: | April 1 Aama, Bouddhanath and Yarchagumba Tea | 43 |
| Chapter 8: | April 2 Pashupati, Thangkas, Momos and Pickle | 59 |
| Chapter 9 | April 3 Swayambhu, Chills and the Kurta Shop | 76 |
| Chapter 10: | April 4 The Egg Shaman, Bhaktapur and Pashmina Shawls | 84 |
| Chapter 11: | April 5 Shopping in Bouddhanath, Lunch with The Chinea Lama & Carpets | 93 |
| Chapter 12: | April 6 The Bandha, Curfew and Erica's Hospitality | 102 |
| Chapter 13: | April 7 Durbar Square and the Yin Yang Restaurant | 107 |
| Chapter 14: | April 8 What We Are Missing and Tagliatelli Verde | 116 |
| Chapter 15: | April 9 Buddha Air to Pokhara, Migmar and Yeshi | 120 |
| Chapter 16: | April 10 Pokhara's Glacier Hotel and Moon Dance | 127 |
| Chapter 17: | April 11 Return to Kathmandu from Pokhara | 134 |
| Chapter 18: | April 12 US Embassy Asks Americans to Evaluate Their Personal Security Posture | 138 |
| Chapter 19: | April 13 Full Moon Shamanic Initiation | 146 |
| Chapter 20: | April 14 Nepali New Year | 158 |
| Chapter 21: | April 15 Confined to the Tibet Guest House | 161 |
| Chapter 22: | April 16 Jeff's Feet Go Shopping, Sano Ram Does Healings and a Chocolate Feast | 162 |
| Chapter 23: | April 17 The Man Chinni Depossession Ceremony | 165 |
| Chapter 24: | April 18 Departing Kathmandu | 176 |
| Chapter 25: | April 18, 19, 20 Three Days, West to East | 179 |
| Chapter 26: | Back In My Real World | 185 |
| | | |
| Book List | | 190 |
| Tibetan Shamanism Workshops led by Dr. Larry G. Peters | | 194 |
| About the Author | | 197 |

# CHAPTER 1
# PRELUDE TO NEPAL

*I think I'm going to Katmandu.
That's really, really where I'm going to.
If I ever get out of here,
That's what I'm gonna do.
K-k-k-k-k-k katmandu.*
                                   Bob Seger

Kathmandu Valley from Swayambhu
(Taken by Mujiba Cabugos)

I became interested in shamanic healing quite by accident the summer of 2000. I had contacted a local healer who made flower essence medicine hoping to incorporate the techniques she used into my own herbal practice. That contact sent me on a whirlwind of experiences and learning. Dana, the flower essence lady, was also a shamanic practitioner and teacher.

Shamanism is a technique in which the practitioner is adept at entering non-ordinary reality to retrieve information. It spans individual religions, so it does not conflict with any individual belief system. The rituals and ceremonies associated with shamanic practice are customized from culture to culture.

As my studies with Dana continued, I learned various methods of healing including extraction, depossession and soul retrieval.

Extraction is the most common healing modality and deals with the removal of intrusions that penetrate a person challenging the balance of their physical and spiritual body. These intrusions are the result of physical, mental or spiritual poisons. Some poisons we bring on ourselves such as anger, lust, pride, ignorance and slothfulness. Others are inserted by sorcery. True sorcerers intend, with full malice of forethought, to use trickery or deception to ruin or rule another. This is called "spoiling" a person. Angry people are usually not full-fledged sorcerers, but they can cause harm by thinking malevolent thoughts. It is also possible to do self-sorcery by harboring feelings of guilt and poor self-esteem. All of these intrusions need to be healed. Extraction is the first step, but sometimes other methods are necessary to free a person of the intrusion.

Depossession is an exorcism type of healing to remove entities, typically ghosts, from the patient.

Soul retrieval is a method by which the shaman goes into non-ordinary reality in search of a piece of the patient's soul that has been sent away or lost. Soul pieces may have become separated in an effort to protect themselves in cases of physical or psychological trauma. The shaman must determine whether the return of the soul piece is appropriate for the patient. Then the soul piece must be healed and then reintegrated. This process can be multi-faceted and may involve various other shamanic techniques, but the object is to move the patient into a better, fuller, more complete life.

I was thirsty for more knowledge and experience, and the shamanic practitioners I met through Dana and her circle were inspiring healers. I was moving quickly along a path I had never expected and it was a very natural progression for me. Perhaps, just perhaps, I was remembering things I already knew from another lifetime.

Then, in a strange turn of events, Dana made a pilgrimage to Mongolia. The experience was, from what I heard through the grapevine, not a good one. The shamanic teacher we knew never returned from Mongolia, her shamanic circle dissolved, she went to work at a gas station and hooked up with a man who did not understand or approve of shamanism, so, at his behest, she turned her back on her gifts forever. Some of us continue to hope that "forever" is a shorter than longer time and that we may yet see Dana emerge as a healer. Those of us who had worked with Dana grieved for her and for our circle. We began to question everything she had taught us, but Chriss, the most devastated of the circle, reminded us that the pre-Mongolia Dana had been a gifted and compassionate teacher. It was as if Dana had died and someone – something – else continued to walk among us wearing her body suit.

A year later, during the bitter Maine winter, I was working with the sled dogs in our kennel. My foot punched through the icy snow crust and sank a foot and a half into the snow just as playful Kodiak barreled into me. I fell sideways but my foot didn't move and I ripped the ligaments around my knee. Surgery was the only option traditional medicine offered. But I knew I could be healed shamanically. One by one I tried to contact Dana's circle, and one by one they indicated that they could not help me. Frustrated, I began asking around since I knew there were other shamanic healers in our area. I located Pat who lives only a stone's throw away from me. She was willing to see me immediately and the ritual she did began the healing process. It just so happened that the following weekend Pat was facilitating a workshop on Tibetan Shamanism with Dr. Larry Peters, an anthropologist from California who had spent over thirty years studying in Nepal. I signed up on the spot.

Sitting in the workshop circle, I discovered I was in the presence of shamanic practitioners with a much wider worldview. They were experienced teachers, authors and gifted healers. Both my knee and my spirit got a tremendous infusion of energy that weekend.

One workshop with Dr. Larry led to another. What interested me was that in the Nepali culture, shamanic healing is mainstream. I was fascinated by the legends and mythology of Nepal and Tibet. And I was building my own shamanic expertise, establishing a working rapport with my spirit guides and using some of the models Larry taught.

On October 13, 2001 my life changed. Larry was conducting a workshop entitled "Soul Retrieval and the Psychopomp Process". Psychopomp is a term given to spiritual assistance rendered to the dead or dying. He led the group through a series of exercises called journeys in which we entered non-ordinary reality and went through the paces a shaman would. There is a process of becoming a shaman that is called "aph-se-aph". By this process a shaman who has died comes to the initiate and requests a funeral. In non-ordinary reality the initiate can make this happen. If the dead shaman is pleased, he/she has the option and ability to transfer all wisdom, knowledge and experience to the initiate. This happened to me.

I had become experienced at entering non-ordinary reality and I was always excited about the messages and experiences I had while journeying. We would lie on the floor with our heads towards the center of our circle and cover our eyes. I used a small pillow of lavender flowers over my eyes because the subtle lavender scent kept me present and prevented me from drifting off to sleep. I was also in the habit of bringing a blanket as my body temperature often dropped during these exercises. Larry would explain where we were to go and what kind of message we were to attempt to retrieve. I loved the tonality of Larry's voice as he directed us to the goals we were seeking. Then Larry would begin to drum. The percussive sound assisted us as we entered non-ordinary reality.

This particular day we were going to see whether we could find an "yi-dam" (pronounced "ee-dam") that might be interested in becoming our guru or teaching spirit.

*JOURNEY:*

I entered non-ordinary reality, which is usually signified by a sense of flying. I also shiver as I enter non-ordinary reality. I found myself in an ancient, arid, hilly terrain. There were rocks and dust and buzzards. I looked about for my yi-dam and saw nothing, no one. Then I remembered that I was looking for someone who was dead and needed a funeral. My first inclination was to look for a cemetery, but there was obviously no cemetery at hand. I then became aware that the shaman I was seeking had been dismembered and his/her body parts were scattered far and wide. I decided to create a "Lui" – an effigy that would serve as a template for bringing together the body parts. In Nepali this effigy is called a "putla" or "gLüd". I carefully drew the image of the Lui in the sand, but the wind blew the sand around and it was difficult to complete the image. I suspected that many times in the past this yi-dam had made contact with various initiates and there was always a distraction – like the wind – that prevented the transfer of knowledge. Dana had taught me a technique for growing plants in an ideal environment. Simplistically, you set up a force field around the seedling providing it with optimum growing conditions. I saw no reason why I could not create a force field around the Lui. It worked! My next task was to collect the body parts and I began an intensive search, at high speed – the speed of thought --, which can only be done in non-ordinary reality. I scanned the landscape and located first one dusty part after another. I lifted each part in my arms, held it to my chest and surrounded it with my heart as I traveled back and forth to the Lui. As the parts were collected the figure of my yi-dam took shape. I thought the yi-dam was a woman at first, but it turned out to be a man who had been castrated. I was worried that I had missed that vital piece, but was given the message that it was never there to be collected.

My would-be yi-dam was very tall, dark-skinned and, as he became animated, dressed in brilliant blue and green flowing robes. He also wore a tall blue, green and gilt headdress, which was the symbol of his highborn estate. He wore a breastplate of precious stones, wristlets and anklets of bells and carried a staff with a shiny black stone on top.

I stood on a ledge above him and asked, "Who are you?"

His reply was not in words but in thoughts – and it felt like wind against my forehead.

He replied: "I am "S...", highborn. We were four. Assassinated. Dismembered. Cast into the desert."

I didn't quite know what to say or think. The first thought that came to my mind was "Am I supposed to create a funeral for you?"

He answered: "You already have. You have taken me into your heart. Retrieved me from the wasteland."

I asked, "Why have you chosen me?"

He continued, "It is time for what I know to be imparted. What I know will not be comprehensible as a block of school learning. It will come to you as needed, in pieces. There is information on world survival, healing, power, and energy. I have approached others in your lineage one after another but they were unwilling, confused, frail or disheartened."

He showed me a fast forward filmstrip of his encounters and I did recognize two family members of older generations.

I queried further, "What does it mean now that you have chosen me?"

He continued, "If there is great upheaval – and I predict there will be – you must do everything in your power to stay safe physically, spiritually, emotionally and intellectually, for the knowledge will be in you. It will reside with you. Do you agree? Are you capable? Are you strong enough, powerful enough? Do you believe?"

I had another question: "I thought that the information I receive in my journeys is from Spirit. How can it be in me?"

My yi-dam laughed – as only a spirit can laugh – in thought transfer that tumbles through the universe like invisible waterfalls.

"And is not Spirit within you?"

This time I laughed.

He said: "I will ask you three times. Three times you must respond. At any time you may choose not to respond."

I nodded and knelt down.

He chanted: "Do you agree? Are you capable? Are you strong enough, powerful enough? Do you believe?"

"Yes, I agree, I am capable, strong and powerful...and I agree to be the vessel of your knowledge. I agree to keep it safe."

He repeated: "Do you agree? Are you capable? Are you strong enough, powerful enough? Do you believe?"

I agreed.

And a third time he asked, and a third time I agreed.

Then he brought his face close to mine – eye to eye – he smelled of sandalwood and his eyes were green. As he gazed into my very soul the knowledge transfer occurred – all wisdom, knowledge and memories transferred. And I realized that I was no longer looking into his green eyes but into a reflection of my own brown eyes.

I felt both exhausted and powerful simultaneously. I was animated. I was also curious about what this special relationship would mean for my life henceforth. I had been chosen. I had accepted. And I knew I had to stay safe.

After the journey was complete, Larry called us back to ordinary reality with a sharp drumbeat and we shared our experiences. This part of the workshop is called "processing". When it was my turn to share I found myself weeping as I related what had just happened. Strangely enough, Dena, sitting to my left, had also seen my yi-dam but more in peripheral vision. Two members of the circle later shared some Judaic tradition, lore and legend with me that seemed to apply. After the workshop Larry gave me the remains of the candle that had been burning on the altar during the weekend.

In non-ordinary reality I had been initiated, and I knew, from reading and intuitively, that a physical crisis would follow. A test! One of my guides warned me that something small and fuzzy would threaten my life.

Back home I was careful as I moved around our rural mountainside property. I was usually diligent in my awareness of my surroundings but I became more so. Our mountain is also home to bears, mountain lions, bobcats and coyotes. They have never bothered us and we live together quite peacefully. Now and then they remind me of their presence with a pile of scat in unexpected places: bobcat scat by the kitchen porch, bear scat near the swimming pool. I know they are there. Smaller critters could also be a threat if they are rabid…and rabies can be a problem around here. I was also exceptionally careful driving in case the "small and fuzzy" should leap out in front of my car. But nothing happened.

My husband is a retired oil tanker captain and now attends vessels as a representative of the owners of the oil cargos. He drives to meet the ships, supervises their off-loading and comes home. His assignments last two to five days and take him from Wilmington, NC to Come-By-Chance, Newfoundland, but are usually in Maine, Massachusetts, New York or New Jersey. During the time frame following my initiation, he was attending a Russian tanker and came home with a virus. He is highly resistant to any kind of illness and shook it off in a couple of days, but by then he had given it to me. This was no ordinary virus and it attacked me with a vengeance. This was probably a microscopic "small and fuzzy".

I was very sick. I lay in bed with a fever that would not break, but not high enough to head for the Emergency Room. I had all the gastro-intestinal symptoms that accompany viruses and I was becoming dehydrated. I rested fitfully and had bizarre dreams and half-waking hallucinations. Sometimes I felt things were crawling on my skin and sometimes I felt a heavy pressure on my chest. After three days I asked Art to get the candle Larry had given me and light it near my bed. The dreams and hallucinations ceased, but the rest of it continued for another four days. During those four days, I was able to meditate and journey and I received interesting insights and messages. I tried to describe them to Art since I was too weak to write it all down.

Of particular relevance was information about an affliction I had been diagnosed with when I was sixteen. I had been falling asleep uncontrollably in class, at dinner and in odd places like standing up on the basketball court, or while counting the measures until my French horn part would begin during orchestra rehearsal. My parents were alarmed. Daddy took me to a specialist at a Boston hospital and after a battery of tests I was diagnosed with narcolepsy with accompanying cataplexy (loss of muscle control in the face and neck). In 1962 it was a brand new discovery and I was an early guinea pig. They began giving me Thyroid medication and then Ritalin. Eventually the drug of choice became Dexedrine and for the next six years I zoomed through life. But during the times when I was not medicated I had discovered that my intuitive powers were becoming increasingly attuned. The drugs were making me edgy, aggressive and I was loosing weight. My mother suggested an alternative: metaphysical healing using Christian Science. I changed my direction and accepted her suggestion. I went off the Dex cold turkey, and, using the principals of Christian Science, established a balance I could live with. The narcoleptic symptoms still overwhelm me if I become overtired or stressed, but the dramatic falling asleep in my mashed potatoes ended. And I had been introduced to spirit healing.

The "small and fuzzy" virus ran its course and I slowly became stronger. As I began to think more clearly I requested an energy work session with my friend Wanda, a skilled healer and teacher, and I got better.

Over the next five years I took every workshop Larry offered and some I took twice. Although I found a shamanic circle nearby, it did not meet my needs, and I eventually met a group in Massachusetts that resonated with me. Whenever I was able, I traveled to journey with them.

I knew Dr. Larry took groups of his students to Nepal. My friend, Carin, had taken the journey in 2002. Jokingly I had told her that if she ever chose to do it again, I would join her, but I never thought I would actually go.

In December 2005 an email from Dr. Larry's number one organizer, his wife, beamed into my computer announcing another trip to Nepal.

## SHAMANIC EXPEDITION AND TRAINING
## NEPAL, SPRING 2006
## (March 29 - April 19, 2006)
## THREE WEEKS OF CULTURAL AND
## SHAMANIC IMMERSION

*Larry Peters, Ph.D. and Sarah Dole will be bringing a small group of participants interested in shamanism and alternate healing methods in a traditional society, to Nepal, to receive shamanic initiations and teachings from master shamans, as well as fully experience the Hindu/Buddhist culture of this beautiful Himalayan kingdom. For more than a decade, Larry Peters has brought hundreds of students to Nepal for this life affirming and change inducing special adventure.*

I booted up Larry's website and read with relish the itinerary of the upcoming trip, assuming I was living the trip vicariously. My husband, Art, made note of the email and said simply, "Do you want to go?" My head reeled and the possibilities opened up. Suddenly I was applying for a passport, filling out paperwork for a Nepali visa and contacting my doctor about inoculations I would need. Art was giving me the most amazing $60^{th}$ birthday present a girl could have!

Nine adventurers signed up for the trip. Two were from Australia. I was the only one from the East Coast, so Dr. Larry's wife, Carol, suggested I fly to California and join the others for the long leg of the journey. She invited me to stay overnight at their house. My flight from the Portland Maine Jetport to Kathmandu was scheduled to lift off March 28. The journey would take three days and I would be moving through Los Angeles, Taipei and Bangkok on the way – all non-Muslim countries, intentionally. As the departure date for our "Three Weeks of Cultural and Shamanic Immersion in Nepal" drew closer, all of us were keeping our eyes on the news and making note of the imminent four-day "bandha", or general strike, that was going to be called on April 6. Our flight was scheduled to touch down in Kathmandu on March 31. I spoke with Larry's wife once and she assured me that Larry would always err on the side of safety, and that was all I needed to know. I had to trust his judgment. Nevertheless, we were all waiting for a trip cancellation right up to the boarding gate.

# CHAPTER 2
## POLITICAL BACKGROUND

To fully understand what was going on in Nepal, it is necessary to understand the background of the political process in the Himalayan kingdom tucked between India and what used to be Tibet. The country is about 500 miles long by 80-150 miles north to south. In 1990 a political movement known as Janaandolan-I...a peoples uprising for democracy and human rights...dismantled the 30-year old Panchayat system, which had been a party-less, absolute monarchy, and heralded the arrival of democracy. The very word democracy seemed to be the answer to all things and most of the people, though not fully understanding what democracy was, were happy.

King Birendra established a constitution, a parliament and a prime minister. But there was a festering Maoist insurgency, especially in the rural areas. There was alleged corruption and patronage, police brutality, drought, and poverty. The geographical position of Nepal makes it a buffer nation between communist China and India. So India anxiously watches the developments in the kingdom while negotiating trade agreements (and disagreements). Nepali history was fraught with change and the repositioning of personalities and parties and power.

Then on June 1, 2001, Nepal leapt into the world headlines when 30-year–old Crown Prince Dipendra, having argued with his parents about his wish to marry, gunned down most of the royal family and then turned the gun on himself. Conspiracy theories abound regarding the palace massacre and everyone in Nepal has their own opinion about what really happened and who was behind it, but the upshot was that it brought Gyanendra, King Birendra's brother, to the throne.

In November 2002, King Gyanendra reacted to increasing Maoist activity and effectively dismissed the government and reinstated palace control of Nepal. The people, organized by the Seven Party Alliance, wanted democracy back. So we were scheduled to land in Kathmandu on the eve of their Janaandolan-II.

# CHAPTER 3
# GATHERING IN LOS ANGELES
## MARCH 28 - 29, 2006

I thought I was organized as I packed over and over again, but it was difficult to know what to bring since there were snow flurries outside my window in Maine and I was anticipating the need for sunscreen, sandals and lightweight shirts.

Footwear was also a big concern. I needed shoes that were easy to remove when entering homes, temples and shrines and would also stand up to mud and rain if necessary. We weren't anticipating trekking, but I knew we would be doing a lot of walking. Merrill or Merrian waterproof shoes were recommended as well as Teva sandals. My first choice would have been a special water sneaker by Solomon that features a heel that collapses into the shoe so you can use it as a slip-on or flip the heel up for better support. But I could not find them. I opted for a rugged pair of black Dansko nursing shoes, my Nikes and a pair of Birkenstock sandals.

The airlines allowed two 60-lb. suitcases, one carry-on and a pocketbook. In retrospect I wish I had taken two huge suitcases to bring back my treasurers, but I settled for my daughter's huge suitcase on wheels, Art's small duffle and a courier-style pack that could accommodate a change of clothing, my camera, Power Bars and a bottle of water. I bought a passport/ticket pouch with a neck lanyard on eBay that I had thought would be a silly extra but it became a lifesaver passing through airports. I would also recommend to anyone traveling that you consider luggage in hot pink or covered with ridiculous patterns to help you recognize your luggage on the baggage carousel. And make sure it has wheels!

Oak Hill Farm had hosted a mammoth pancake breakfast and sugarhouse open house two days before my flight left, so I was still mopping up syrup details as I finalized my packing. In days of yore I would have gotten a blue ribbon for organization, packing exactly what I needed and having it all checked and rechecked. This time I barely passed Stowage

101 and would never have gotten the task done had Art not stepped in.

Art was becoming anxious as we drove to Portland. What dryer setting should he use for dungarees? How much soap should he use for a load of laundry? Where were the packing boxes for shipping maple syrup? Where were the vacuum cleaner bags? How would he know spam on the computer? And various other tidbits he would have to know during his three-week bachelorhood.

We said a cuddly goodbye and I was OFF on my adventure of a lifetime. I flew Delta from Portland to Cincinnati and then Cincinnati to Los Angeles. There wasn't much to do on the seven-hour flight. The plane was not full so I had a whole row of seats to myself, and no one to talk with. The in-flight movie was "Cheaper By The Dozen 2" which was an immediate "No, thank you". Delta is in bankruptcy so there were random snacks, but no real meals. I read magazines and dozed and stared into the black night sky wondering what lay ahead.

I had brought three books with me, Michael Harner's "The Way of the Shaman", Andrew Weil's "Healthy Aging" and Richard Roberts "I Was Much Happier When Everything I Owned Was in the Back Seat of My Volkswagen". I never opened one of them.

Larry's wife met me about 10:30 PM at LAX.

With her was Sarah Dole, the co-captain of the adventure. Sarah had flown down from Sebastopol, CA near San Francisco.

Sarah and I were overnight guests at the Peters' compound in Topanga, CA. The massive gate that keeps their three dogs (plus two grand-dogs) in is painted with a glorious dragon stretched across the full 12 feet of it. The dogs tumbled out to meet us – tiny Bella, a chubby white Chihuahua, affectionate Tigger, and timid Bear who is a cross between a Golden Retriever, a Rhodesian Ridgeback and a Great Pyrenees. We moved through the house, which was a veritable museum of Nepali Thangkas (sacred wall hangings), sculpture and carpets. We were tired and there was time in the morning to visit. Carol's evening FAX from Larry had just arrived and it was clear she wanted to curl up alone with the message. Larry writes Carol a letter – a love letter – every day and faxes it to her from wherever he is in the world. It is one of the secrets to their long and passionate marriage. I left Carol in the living room and retired to their daughter Jemma's room and was asleep as soon as my head hit the pillow.

Carol Peters is in the rock and roll business. Her current hot property is a group called "Heart" (Remember "Dreamboat Annie"? "Magic Man"?) but she handles several others as well. Her Christian rock group was supposed to be en route from Nashville to Minneapolis and she received a call in the night that their bus had broken down (I think the wording was "Blown up!"). Carol's staff arrived and set up shop around the dining room table, each addressing pressing problems on their laptops while Carol ironed out transportation for the stranded Christian rock and rollers. Wearing her telephone headset, and carrying on at least two conversations at once, she managed to make us breakfast, make coffee for her staff, feed the dogs and get Sarah and I out the door and on our way to meet the other five adventurers at the airport. Somewhere along the line she had managed to bake cookies for Larry and we tucked them into my suitcase.

The route from Topanga Canyon to the airport took us along the beach. I had never seen the Pacific Ocean before. At an intersection Carol rolled down her window to give a homeless man a couple of dollars. She knew by sight the panhandlers who made a career of standing on the corner, but this guy was new.

Near the international check-in Carol identified and corralled Denise from Oregon, Erica from Tucson, Susan from Minneapolis, Mujiba from Santa Barbara and Jeff from Seattle. Carol had the advantage of having handled all our passports when she sent for our Nepali visas. But who looks like their passport picture? I guess we all did! Sarah became our Mother Hen and we promptly became her six peeps. We fell into a hurry-up-and-wait mode. Most of the waiting was done in slowly moving lines. We moved through security, check-in and yet another layer of security. As we stood in one line after another at LAX we had time to talk and people watch.

# CHAPTER 4
# MY FELLOW ADVENTURERS

It amazes me that not one of us thought to take a group picture. So let me introduce you to our travelers individually.

*Sarah Dole*
*(Taken by Mujiba Cabugos)*

Sarah is a shamanic practitioner and teacher. Her flowing silver hair was often pinned up, but she could have been the poster child for anti-Clairol baby boomers everywhere. From 1969 to 2001, she lived in the Ramagiri Ashram in Tomales, CA. The meditation practice of ashram life involved living and working with the 50 people who made up the ashram family. While Sarah was part of the community she helped cook vegetarian meals for the group and was active in the publication and hand binding of a vegetarian cookbook called "Laurel's Kitchen". Sarah left the ashram when she began to study and practice shamanic healing. She has studied intensively with Michael Harner's Foundation for Shamanic Studies, completing the three-year program in Advanced Shamanism and Shamanic Healing. She traveled to Nepal for the first time with Larry in 2002. The next year, she joined a group in Brazil to attend a workshop on "Medicine for the Earth" presented by Sandra Ingerman. This trip included a two-week visit with John of God, a respected medium who performs healings. Sarah's latest course of study is with Sandra Ingerman participating in her two-year teacher training on Shamanic Journeying and Healing. Sarah has also experienced Bear Medicine with Carol Proudfoot. Besides her healing work, Sarah likes to make jewelry to sell and has a keen eye for unusual beads and facets. There were a lot of beadwork vendors we might never have paid attention to if it were not for Sarah. Sarah often wore saris and was on the lookout for exceptional textiles, especially silks. Sarah's son will be getting married at about the same time as my daughter, Krissie, so we had the commonality of being wedding planners. Sarah and her husband split up before she left the ashram and she is now seeing a man named John whom she spoke of warmly with that hooded sparkle one gets when everything is still new and wonderful and you can't quite believe it.

*Mujiba Cabugos*
(Taken by Sue Melanson)

Mujiba Cabugos is a petite, sparkly Filipino lady from Santa Barbara, CA. Chronologically she is probably middle-aged, but her youthful spirit, clear eyes and smooth dark skin make her one of those ageless people whose actual age can never quite be ascertained. She is an RN with a holistic healing practice that includes shamanic healing, massage and homeopathic remedies. She is deeply connected to her Philippine heritage and changed her given name to Mujiba because it fit better. She is well read and familiar with Buddhist practice and sacred texts, and she is a skilled musician. She celebrates the divine feminine through music (voice, piano and tambura) and is a member of three vocal groups: Moving Breath is a five woman a-capella group, Zaremaya is comprised of two members from Moving Breath, and Tingsha is a six member group performing vibrational sound journeys oriented towards meditation. Their music is released through Heartway Muse and includes four albums: "She Changes" by

Moving Breath, "She Dreams" by Moving Breath, "Call To Here And Now" by Tingsha, and "Seeing Sound, Hearing Color" by Zaremaya. Mujiba and her husband, Patrick McAvoy, are avid kayakers. But kayaking also robbed her of her brother. Mujiba and Patrick created a Lost At Sea Memorial at the east end of the Santa Barbara breakwater in honor of her brother, Ted, who was lost at sea kayaking off Leadbetter Beach. They donated the memorial, which includes a dolphin, two whale tail benches and a compass rose, to the City of Santa Barbara. Over the course of our adventure we all got to hear about the heart-connections that were being carried with each of us to Kathmandu. Mujiba's daughter, Leyla, is presently traveling as part of a five-month study of endangered plants in Southeast Asia and India. Leyla was very close to Mujiba wherever we went.

*Erica Swadley*
*(Taken by Sue Melanson)*

Erica Swadley is from Tucson, Arizona, a 1962 graduate of RISD (Rhode Island School of Design) - which, if you do the math - made her the oldest in our group. Erica is 66. She is an accomplished artist and shamanic practitioner. She often writes poetry to accompany her brightly colored oils and monotypes. Erica's contemporary work is filled with an ethereal quality, using symbolism in her art not just as an intellectual exercise but also as an expression of a personal belief system. Sometimes she incorporates Hindu iconography into her works. Erica emanates a gentle excitement about the world in general and although she speaks softly she could come up with irreverent humor to rival the best of us. She wears a silver Ganesh pendant (the elephant headed deity) and is particularly connected to Hanuman, a Hindu monkey deity known for his dedication to righteousness, performance of entrusted duties, and unfailing talents in serving his chosen master. At home her husband, Virgil, had ordered license plates for her car that said "Hanumom" – a cutesy take-off on Erica's connection to the deity. Erica is a lover. She loves people, the deities, the rocks and hills and trees, and she made the most of whatever we encountered. Erica is the epitome of the cup-is-half-full gal, only Erica would also imbue the cup with sparkles, delicious flavor, aromatherapy and a goodly dose of magic.

*Susan Langston*
(Taken by Mujiba Cabugos)

Susan Langston has a psychiatric practice in Minneapolis that incorporates shamanic healing, Reiki and EMDR (Eye Movement Desensitization and Reprocessing). Often she works with trauma and sexual abuse victims. Susan is a tiny woman of enormous stature. But that I mean she is extremely high energy, openly genuine and emotionally right at the surface. Susan was a total joy to live with - consistently and increasingly. Susan noticed things the others missed and was attentive to all the rest of us. Sarah was the official Mother Hen designee, but Susan was the keeper of all of us, including Sarah. She lives in Minnesota with her partner, Gail. They are both musical, and the night Gail was playing a gig Susan was very tuned in and aware when Gail was performing. Susan did more than sparkle - she effervesced! Throughout the trip Susan Langston was always referred to as "Susan" and the author as "Sue".

*Jeff Romberger*
(Taken by Mujiba Cabugos)

Jeff Romberger from Kirkland, Washington is an energy efficiency engineer who does diagnosis on really big projects, such as Seattle's utilities. Besides his day job he is a shamanic practitioner and an Aloha Mana Lomi Lomi Massage practitioner. He is also a runner. Jeff is recently divorced after twenty-five years of marriage and he maintains a warm, friendly relationship with his ex-wife. He says she is his best friend. They have a son and a daughter in their early twenties. He is presently living in an apartment but will be looking for a house as soon as he returns from Nepal. His personal life is in flux, and so is his sense of home. Nevertheless, he embraces the world with optimism and a sense of humor. Jeff was very much at ease in our band of women and we enjoyed his company. Jeff is eloquent and has a way of summing up and stating what we were all feeling in any given moment. He has compassion and sensitivity towards everyone he encounters... store clerks with whom he made bartering an enjoyable game, dining room staff whom he made sure knew how much he appreciated their efforts, and little children on the street whom he responded to playfully when all the rest of us were just annoyed with their presence.

*Denise Shepherd*
(Taken by Sue Melanson)

Denise Shepherd is a homeopathic healer and shamanic practitioner from Coos Bay, Oregon, who also helps facilitate vision quests in Death Valley. Her homeopathic training takes her to England regularly and she is incredibly gifted at being able to intuitively prescribe exactly what a patient needs no matter how difficult the diagnosis or how unusual the cure. She works with the whole spectrum of homeopathic cures. She recently moved her entire life, including four horses, from Ohio to Oregon. Her husband is ex-military, considerably older than she is and has health problems. She has raised three sons who are all on their own now and have given her several grandbabies that are in her thoughts and conversation daily. Her passion in life is endurance horse racing, which is quite a feat. To have a horse that has the ability, endurance and nerve to win an endurance race is one thing; to have the horsemanship to make the horse win is another. Denise has both. Because Denise and I come by our shamanic abilities in much the same way, we gravitated towards one another. We understood that a direct line to Spirit gets the information clearer and faster than a long resume of workshops, apprenticeships and book learning. Denise indicated that the directive she received from her guides to accompany this group to Nepal was to socialize her. Denise is very probably one of the key reasons I was guided to be a part of this group.

*June Winston-Smith and Burt Hambright*
*(Taken by Mujiba Cabugos)*

June Winston-Smith and Burt Hambright, the Australian newlyweds, were a puzzlement. We never really got a feel of who they were, what they do, or why they were with us. They were pleasant and polite (for the most part) but very withdrawn and isolated. They had met at a shamanic workshop. Burt was from the United States and had once taught at a farm extension school. His disdain for the US government managed to come up in just about every conversation. June was from Perth, Australia. After they were married Burt expatriated to Australia. They had arrived in Kathmandu several days before we did and enjoyed the advantage of having one of Larry's staff at their disposal as they explored the city on their own.

# CHAPTER 5
# MARCH 29 - 30, 2006
# THE FINAL LEG OF THREE DAYS OF TRAVEL

On board the China Air flight 005 from LAX to Taipei, Mujiba, Denise and I sat three across while Sarah, Susan and Erica faced the bulkhead. Jeff had a window seat to himself. And so we embarked on the fourteen-hour flight across the Pacific.

I had been quite anxious about being as broad of girth as I am for the flight. I was afraid I wouldn't fit in the seat, but I did. I was afraid the seatbelt would not go around me, but they offered me an extender. But the thing I had not anticipated was that my tray table would not go down fully over my lap. So I learned to balance it on my knees. I was beginning to feel like a second-class citizen until I realized that Denise had the same problems. So she and I were perfect seatmates...thighbone to thighbone across the ocean blue.

We had little TV screens on the back of the seat in front of us and, using headsets, we could select movies – I dozed off to "Fun With Dick and Jane" and woke up in the middle of "The Family Stone". On one channel we could watch the progress of the flight on a map. We arched north across the Aleutian Islands and then down towards Japan – somewhere along the way we crossed the International Date Line. Two other channels accessed cameras on the underbelly and the nose of the plane.

Denise and I took the opportunity to stand up and walk around every time one or the other of us had to use the restroom. The flight attendants came around with water on a regular basis to keep us hydrated. Although alcoholic beverages were complimentary, all the China Air literature stressed staying away from caffeine and alcohol to prevent dehydration. In the compact bathrooms pump bottles of aromatherapy moisture lotion were available.

We switched planes in Taipei and had time for a quick bathroom break. Then on to Bangkok, which was two hours away. We crossed over the Vietnam peninsula and I felt like I was passing over an historical site...or perhaps an historical graveyard. I read the names of the major cities and each conjured up names of people who had died in or near them. People I once knew. Gene Daly and Dana Frost had to endure a flight just as long as the one I was experiencing in order to drop into the jungles to fight and die...so long ago, and yet I could remember. Gene had been laid to rest near the family's summer home on Cape Cod. I knew the undertaker in Naples, Maine had been requested to open Dana's casket before they lowered it into his grave...just to be certain the body was Dana's. Mistakes like that happened during the Viet Nam War. But it was Dana and he is buried in Maine.

Bangkok was sweltering hot and it was after 1 AM their time when we landed. We had reservations at the Amari Hotel. Sarah decided we should all exchange money in a machine so we would have enough Baht to pay the exit tax when we left the next day. I tried to change $30 US and discovered that the airport money changing machines did not recognize the new US holographic bills. Susan loaned me some Baht and I found an in-person Money Changer the next day.

The hotel was connected to the airport by a walkway bridge. All of us were tired and cranky and in need of a shower. We turned to our Mother Hen who was wandering around the Bangkok airport looking for the words "Amari Hotel". Eventually we found it.

Denise and I were paired as roommates and gasped when we walked into our room to see a king size bed, until we realized it was actually two twins pushed together. We showered, brushed our teeth with bottled water and fell into bed. Being prone was such a luxury!

Carol Peters had raved about the breakfast buffet in the Amari's Zeppelin Restaurant. She had said she would travel all the way to Bangkok just for that breakfast buffet. But Sarah thought it was too pricey and the group headed back into the airport to find somewhere to eat. Around and around we went, luggage in tow. Looking, trying to decide. I just wanted coffee!

We ended up in an airport style café that served good strong American coffee. Most of the group was trying to decipher the menu when Erica had the brilliant idea to point-and-pick her own breakfast from the brightly lit bakery case. We still don't know exactly what it was she picked, but it looked good. Mujiba was the gourmet adventurer of the group and ordered a spicy soup and tarot root in coconut milk. The rest of us used the point-and-order system, and eventually, we all got fed. In retrospect, the Zeppelin buffet would have been easier, and after all was said and done, Jeff picked up the tab for everyone.

Our Thai Air flight left for Kathmandu at 10:30 AM. We had time to get to the gate, discover it was the wrong one, reconnoiter, and eventually get to where we needed to be.

Denise had the choice right hand window seat, which was the desirable position for viewing the Himalayas...including Mt. Everest...as they came into view.

Kathmandu is a city of about 720,000 people nestled in a smog-covered valley. The tallest buildings are no more than seven or eight stories and many of the streets are so narrow they are only passable by foot traffic. A number of smoke stacks on the outskirts belched heavy black smoke into the air. We later learned that these were brick factories.

As observed from above, the Kathmandu Valley is designed as a mandala or elliptical circle within the surrounding rim of mountain peaks. It is a melting pot of all the major Eastern religions. Within the valley, shrines and temples identify the power places, or residences, of important deities. For Newari Buddhists, the Swayambhu shrine overlooking Kathmandu dominates the valley. For Tibetan Buddhists, the Bouddhanath stupa is most important. For Hindus, Pashupati is worshipped as the residence of Shiva. At the confluences of rivers you will find the power places of the Mother Goddesses as well as the major residences of the Naga water-spirits.

And here I was, descending in my great shiny flying bird, about to embark on an explorative journey. I had come to play with the deities on their turf, in their places of power.

# CHAPTER 6
# MARCH 31, 2006 FRIDAY
# ARRIVAL IN KATHMANDU

Around noon Thai Air touched down, and a rolling staircase came to meet the plane. The terminal was modern and air-conditioned and it surrounded us with a sense of terracotta, marble and a tasteful ambiance. A large animated billboard displayed first a view of a pub called Rum Doodle then a picture of the Tibet Guest House where we were headed. I was impressed! Customs and passport control were fast and efficient. We collected our luggage and then the fun began.

In our "Nepal Travel Tips", Larry had warned us not to let anyone who was not affiliated with the Tibet Guest House touch our suitcases. We stepped out of the terminal and were besieged by an army of "helpers" trying to maneuver our luggage hither and yon. One man got right in my face and said, in plain English, "Tibet Guest House". It took me a minute to realize that he was simply mimicking what he had heard Sarah loudly announce. I clenched my luggage with white knuckled determination. Sarah had located the Tibet Guest House van and legitimate helpers were loading our bags onto the roof rack.

A stray dog was sleeping under the van and one of the porters kicked him to make him move. It joggled my sensibilities to see someone kick a dog, but I soon learned that stray dogs are everywhere and are not safe to touch because of disease and rabies. Eventually I convinced myself that they were as common as squirrels in the US.

We tumbled into the van and held our breath for the thrill ride of a lifetime. Nepali traffic does not even begin to compare with Boston at rush hour. They drive on the left and they honk their horns a lot. Squeezing by other vehicles with fractions of inches to spare is commonplace. Beside tourist vehicles there were motorcycles, bikes, rickshaws and taxis. One fleet of taxis is the size of VW bugs and are called Tuk Tuk Taxis.

Art had been concerned that I might suffer altitude sickness, but Kathmandu sits at about 4500 ft. above sea level, and I had no problem.

I was also braced for unfamiliar and possibly stomach wrenching smells, but I was pleasantly surprised to discover that the city has a pungent incense smell everywhere you go. There were occasions when I would come around a corner and a foul smell would surprise me, but for the most part, dirty city that it is, the smells were tolerable. It is also good luck for shopkeepers to burn incense in their stores to bring good spirits. I had brought facemasks recommended by a friend. Technol Fluid-Shield Procedure Masks, #47107 are produced by Kimberly-Clark and are latex free. I had to order them through my dentist and I did use them on particularly dusty days.

*Traffic in Kathmandu*
(Taken by Mujiba Cabugos)

As we maneuvered, at breakneck speed, from the airport to the Thamel district I tried to take in everything I could. A festival that had something to do with horses was going on and required that we detour around it. The city was bustling with activity. Construction workers, some of them women wearing saris, stood in lines handing bricks and buckets of concrete along human chains to the actual building site. Sidewalk vendors were everywhere supplying produce, staples, clothing and even "Rolex" watches to the masses. Miniature neighborhood shrines dotted the city. Underfed cows roamed freely and we passed a small family of goats tied to a telephone pole. Roaster carts sold popcorn and soybeans, freshly heated and ready to snack on. Young men rode bicycles with sheets stretched between the handlebars carrying artistically arranged carrots and unfamiliar root vegetables. Laundry hung from balconies and saris drying in the afternoon sun hung a story and a half down the sides of buildings like colorful banners. Intricately carved doorways, window grates and roof details bespoke the age and artistic skill of Kathmandu's creators. The shops we passed had open fronts to the sidewalks with overhead garage-door style galvanized curtains that closed them in at night. The women we saw wore traditional saris or kurtas (dresses with matching punjab pants and coordinating shawls) or western jeans and tee shirts. We did not see bare midriffs, shorts or tank tops, except on tourists. The men dressed in western jeans and shirts and sneakers or sandals. Some wore fez style hats or baseball caps. Children with bright smiles and big curious eyes played in doorways, the older ones caring for the younger. The littlest were often dressed only in shirts to save on diapers as they were being potty trained.

    We turned into a tidy courtyard at the Tibet Guest House and were ushered inside with great warmth and hospitality. The staff are always happy to see Dr. Larry's people. Larry met us with smiles and hugs and happy reunions. I had not realized how very long it had been since I had seen my dear teacher and friend.

*Dr. Larry Peters*
*(Taken by Sue Melanson)*

We checked in and our luggage was sent ahead to our rooms, then we sat together in a corner of the lobby and the staff brought us tea – black tea or milk tea, which was actually a masala spice tea. We had arrived in our home away from home, and it felt like home – a safe oasis in a strange bustling city. Off the lobby is a cool shady restaurant with a sunny garden terrace. An Internet room is located near the front desk and that would be my link to home.

As a welcome gift Larry presented each of us with a Rittha seed mala (prayer beads) in a silk mala bag. Shamans use these malas for prayer, divination and extraction work.

Sarah was obviously stressed and was trying to accomplish a mental checklist. One of the things she wanted to do was be sure everyone had a buddy. The buddy system was a great idea in an even-numbered group but we were a group of nine. Somehow I became the odd man out. I asked Sarah what I should do about this lack-of-buddy situation and she snapped back "Why don't you ask someone else." Susan overheard the interchange and patted me on the back whispering, "She's just overloaded."

Dr. Larry always stays in the penthouse apartment where he has his own living quarters and kitchen. His suite opens onto a large sheltered deck that overlooks the city and became our usual meeting place, but that first day we agreed to meet in the lobby after getting settled and unpacked.

Room 304 was my assigned living space. Erica was across the hall and Susan two doors down. Poor Susan was having separation anxiety after we had been wedged into such close proximity for two days. She sensed the vast unfriendliness of Room 306's unknown occupant who lived between us. My room had windows on two sides, one bank overlooking a garden where a didgeridoo was playing and the other overlooking the alley. I had two twin beds with foam mattresses mounted on plywood frames that were just this side of comfortable. The room had an ingenious single unit piece of furniture that incorporated a desk, dressing table and mirror, luggage rack, wall pegs for hanging clothing and a cupboard.

*Tibet Guest House Room 304*
(Taken by Sue Melanson)

My bathroom would have been described as "dated" in the US. But in Nepal it was first class. We had to rely on "mineral water" (bottled water) for everything including brushing our teeth. We were warned not to sing in the shower in case we should take in an unwanted mouthful of tainted water. I hadn't brought a hair dryer, but if I had I would have needed an outlet adaptor. I had also forgotten a clock and there was none in the room.

I partially unpacked, took a quick satisfying shower and changed from the clothes I had been wearing since California. I've never held to the cliché that clothes make the woman, but clean clothes certainly help.

The group gathered in the lobby. We stuck our heads into the computer room to discover that a half hour of Internet time would cost 20 rupees. We all thought that was outrageous until we figured out that 20 rupees is the equivalent of 30 cents US.

Larry's staff joined us for dinner. His handpicked helpers became our interpreters, bartering advocates and, although it wasn't widely advertised, they were also our bodyguards. Over the next few weeks they also became our Nepali family.

*Ram Sapkota*
*(Taken by Sue Melanson)*

Ram Sapkota is a distinguished Brahman (high caste Nepali) in his early 50's with salt and pepper hair. He is a gentleman farmer and owns a farm in a remote village. When he is acting as staff for Dr. Larry's people he stays in the Bouddhanath district of Kathmandu with his son Pramod's family. Both Pramod and his sister have presented Ram with grandchildren, and his role as grandfather is a proud one. His other son is studying to be a doctor, an orthopedist, in Beijing, China. He watched over us carefully, taking note of times when we needed to rest or when one of our group dropped behind. Ram is a remarkably sensitive, observant and compassionate guide as well as a skilled barterer and interpreter.

*Pramod Sapkota*
*(Taken by Sue Melanson)*

Pramod Sapkota is Ram's handsome 29-year-old son. He speaks very good English and has a sparkle and wit that picked up on most of our Western humor. Pramod is politically outspoken and, if he stays in Nepal, that may get him into a lot of trouble. He has a network of friends all over Kathmandu who stay in touch by cell phone and this proved helpful to all of us during the political unrest in the city. He had his phone on the pulse of the city. Pramod knows a great deal about Kathmandu and I suspect that were we ever in a tight situation that required immediate departure, he would know the obscure alleyways and courtyards to accomplish it. He has just finished college, is newly married and has a new baby, and he is restless. His whole life lies ahead of him and he is anxious to get on with it.

*Gauri*
*(Taken by Mujiba Cabugos)*

Gauri is a short compact fellow with a broad smile and eyes that dance. He owns a couple of shops in the Thamel district of Kathmandu, one being a high-end Thangka studio. He is a gifted businessman with a trained eye for quality artisan work. His ambition is to extend his entrepreneurial ventures to the United States.

*Jigme Lama*
*(Taken by Mujiba Cabugos)*

Jigme Lama is the son of the Chinea Lama, who is a political/religious leader of the Bouddhanath area. Jigme runs a carpet factory. He has a wealth of knowledge, but, as we discovered with time, some of it may be myth. He is in outstanding physical shape and probably is older than he looks. He does physical daily meditation exercises (prostrations) and has practiced martial arts most of his life. He is proud of his country, proud to be a Buddhist and proud of his remarkable carpets. Jigme's powers of observation, his intense interest in everything and everyone around him, as well as his ability to think outside the box made me, personally, feel that I could trust this man with my life.

*Sano Ram*
(Taken by Sue Melanson)

Sano Ram is a skilled shaman having been taken and trained by the Bon Jankrit (yeti) as a child. He cannot speak English but communicates easily thru the others. Sano Ram is soft spoken and a little shy, a gentle man with a wealth of shamanic knowledge and experience to share with our group.

*Suju*
(Taken by Sue Melanson)

Suju is our driver. He and Pramod are reflections of one another and they often break into their native tongue forgetting we are there. Suju manages to maneuver the modern, air-conditioned 20-seater bus through the narrowest streets and the toughest traffic jams.

Larry had planned an authentic Newari dinner at a restaurant to kick off our experience. We walked through the Thamel district on the way to the restaurant. Thamel is considered a "tourist ghetto" and is full of artisan and trekker supply shops, restaurants of all sorts and hotels. It is tightly compact, full of activity and noise and traffic. Merchants smile and nod "Namaste", the typical "Good Day" greeting, as we pass, hoping we will stop to browse. There were intriguing shops selling jewelry, textiles, clothing, wood sculpture, crystals, wall hangings, bronze singing bowls, sacred objects, odd carved musical instruments and drums. People are everywhere on the brick and cobblestone streets and we had to hug the edge of the streets to keep from being run down by traffic.

The Thamel Restaurant is in an ancient house, with wood-carved windows and doors. The beamed ceilings and old plaster walls are whitewashed. Jigme filled us in on the content of the plaster, which is called "leun". It is made from rice husks, cow dung and soil. Larry reserved the second floor dining room, which has a long low (twelve inches off the floor) table, floor pillows and atmospheric candlelight. As became our custom throughout our stay, before entering the dining room itself, we removed our street shoes and left them on racks provided for that purpose. I found the floor pillow layout difficult after all the plane time. We began the meal with a spicy appetizer made principally of roasted soybeans. Dal-Bhat-Tarkari is a staple in Nepal and that came next. Dal is a lentil soup, Bhat is plain rice and Tarkari is a vegetable curry in a broth. Bandel Tareko is fried wild boar and Alo Tareko is traditional fried potatoes very much like our French Fries. The attentive waiters served shallow pottery cups of Rakshi, potent firewater made from rice. We sampled momos, which are steamed dumplings filled with chopped meat or vegetables served with a dipping concoction they called "pickle". Jigme told us pickle is to "brighten up your mouth" and is made with tomatoes, radish, coriander and boiled, diced potatoes. The last thing I sampled before indulging in a second Rakshi, was a portion of curried meat that was either buff (water buffalo) or mutton. After that second Rakshi it really didn't matter what I was eating.

    That first night I fell asleep with a strange, spiced coating on my tongue that no amount of Colgate was going to rinse off. Our cultural immersion had begun.

## CHAPTER 7
## April 1, 2006 SATURDAY
## AAMA, BOUDDHANATH AND YARCHAGUMBA TEA

We began our first day with breakfast. The dining room was shady and cool and welcoming. Every linen-draped table in the dining room was adorned with an Amaryllis blossom in a bud vase. Ornately carved and painted ceiling trim matched the massive bar along the back wall. A framed aerial view of Tibet's City of Llasa dominated another wall. We had the option of eating in the adjacent garden, but congregated inside instead. We read local newspapers as we ate, and glanced at the news on the TV in the corner. There was talk about the bandha (strike) scheduled for April 6, but no one seemed terribly concerned. Transportation strikes happen in Nepal. We would just work around it.

Sarah had warned us that coffee lovers will not be satisfied with the beverage they call coffee, and, indeed, Sarah was right. We ordered coffee and received awkward little metal pots full of something akin to weak Nescafe. I discovered Hot Lemon, which is nothing more than a half a lemon squeezed into boiling water. That became my morning beverage. Dense white bread toast is served with either honey or jelly, and the jelly is always cherry. I liked it, but I knew Art would have wanted something different.

Our plan of the day was to travel to Aama's home to observe her morning healing rituals, after which we would finally meet her. After spending the morning with Aama, we would be introduced to the Bouddhanath neighborhood, which includes the stupa and surrounding environs.

Suju had backed the bus as close to the courtyard as possible and we clambered on board carrying everything we THOUGHT we needed for a day's outing. Each day our daypacks became lighter as we discovered what we truly did not need. One of our most important daypack items was bottled water. The mesh pocket on my daypack was designed for a water bottle but not for the standard liter bottles we found everywhere in Nepal. Erica had come prepared with a crocheted water bottle carrier that fit the large bottles with no problem.

By way of orientation, the Ring Road runs around the city. Kantipath is a north-south road that cuts right through the heart of Kathmandu. At the northern end of Kantipath is the king's palace. The Thamel tourist district, where we were staying, is just west of the palace. Durbar Square is at the very center of Kathmandu. Bouddhanath is just outside the northeast corner of the Ring Road. Aama's home and the Bouddhanath Stupa are located there. Just south of Bouddhanath is the Hindu cremation site of Pashupati on the banks of the Bagmati River. South of Pashupati lies the Tribhuvan International Airport, our point of entry. To the west is Swayambhu. The Swayambhu stupa is visible, on clear days, from Larry's rooftop garden. Tribhuvan University is south of Swayambhu. Along the southern section of the Ring Road is the City of Patan, and the ancient city of Bhaktapur lies east of Patan.

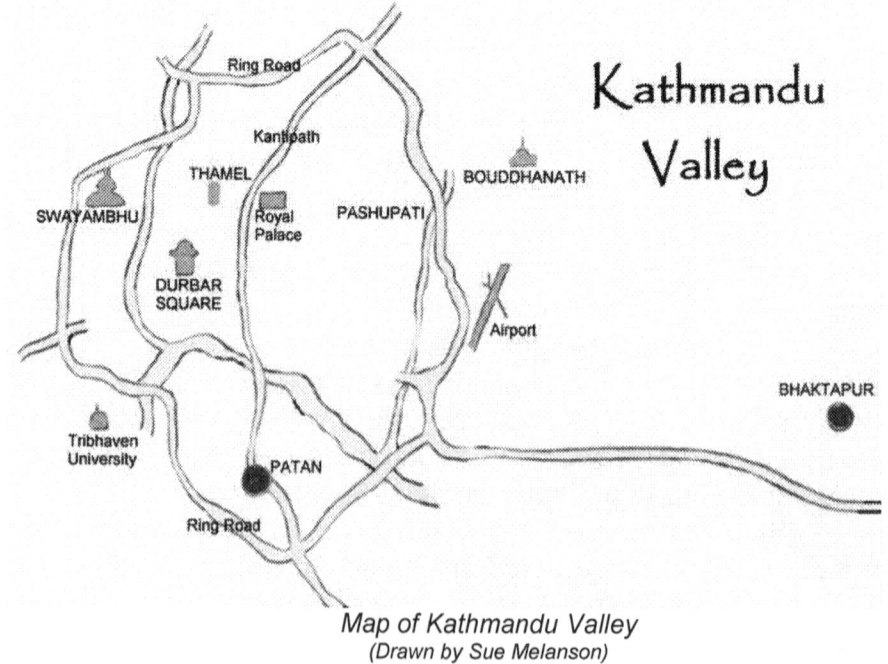

Map of Kathmandu Valley
(Drawn by Sue Melanson)

A couple of blocks from the hotel, Larry had Suju stop the bus beside the local Ganesh Shrine.

Ganesh is the Hindu elephant-headed deity, one of the sons of Shiva and Parvoti. The story goes that Shiva was away when Ganesh was born and didn't know about the blessed event. When Shiva returned, Ganesh had grown and was standing guard over his mother's chambers. Ganesh did not know Shiva, nor did Shiva know Ganesh, so, naturally, dutiful Ganesh refused to allow Shiva to enter. This infuriated Shiva and he lopped off Ganesh's head. Parvoti appeared and was heartbroken that Shiva had killed their son. Being deities, Parvoti knew that if she grieved loudly enough Shiva would have to do something. In a moment of panic Shiva seized the first living animal to pass by...an elephant...and he replaced Ganesh's head with that of the elephant. Ganesh is known as the Lord of Beginnings and the Lord of Wisdom and all Hindus begin worship by asking for his blessing. It is said that he will remove gannas (obstacles) from your way, so it is a very wise thing to approach him before beginning any endeavor, including entering into your daily routine. So on the first day of our Nepali adventure it was particularly appropriate that we invoke his blessing.

*Sarah receives tika at the Ganesh shrine*
*(Taken by Sue Melanson)*

Each one of us slipped out of our street shoes and knelt before the little shrine, laying a few rupees on the offering plate. The shrine keeper gave us tika – a red ochre dot on the forehead that temporarily anchored a couple of pieces of rice to the spot. We then circumambulated the little shrine. Circumambulation is a religious exercise whereby the meditator walks clockwise around a shrine or other holy spot, ringing bells and spinning prayer wheels. In Eastern mythology most of the deities have a specified "vehicle", or animal on which they ride. Ganesh rides a mouse that is capable of gnawing through even the most difficult obstacles.

*Ganesh's vehicle, the Mouse*
*(Taken by Mujiba Cabugos)*

In a tiny hole in the brick wall opposite the Ganesh shrine is a stone mouse about the size of a fat Chihuahua. The faithful had put red ochre tika on the statue as well as flower petals.

On our quest to observe and learn from various shamans, our first stop was Aama Bombo's healing room in Bouddhanath.

*Police in Kathmandu, watching and waiting*
(Taken by Mujiba Cabugos)

On the way to Aama's, we passed the king's palace. We could see police in blue fatigues armed with bamboo batons, and more formidable army regulars, clad in brown fatigues, leaning on barricades made of sandbags or strolling cautiously among the passers by. There was a definite tension in the air.

The bus parked at the bottom of Aama's street. On the corner was the neighborhood laundromat, which was a sunken stone courtyard with water coming out of an ornately carved spout. Women pounded their laundry on the stones and rinsed them under the stone spigot. Across the dusty ally was a ghat. Hindus burn their dead on stone platforms called ghats and the ashes are thrown into tributaries of the sacred Ganges River. This ghat had a roof overhead giving it the look of an ornate gazebo.

A herd of lean water buffalo was penned beyond the laundry area and a tiny woman passed us carrying a bale of clover on her back intended for the buffs. The clover was contained in a piece of rough fabric attached to a strap the woman wore around her forehead. Little brown children, curious about this band of foreigners, followed us up the dirt ally to Aama's. They smiled and called to us "Hello, hello" and when we responded in kind they screeched with delight.

*Aama Bombo*
*(Taken by Mujiba Cabugos)*

Aama Bombo is a warm, compassionate, gifted healer. She is 67 years old and has been practicing shamanism for almost forty years. Her reputation for healing and divination is widely known and she recently became one of The International Council of Thirteen Indigenous Grandmothers. There is an ancient prophecy, shared by indigenous tribes all over the world, that states that at a crucial time in human history, when the world is on the brink of total destruction, the Grandmothers of all the worlds tribes will unite in an alliance of prayer, education and healing for Mother Earth, her inhabitants, and the children of the next seven generations to come. That time has come.

Aama is a highly respected shaman in a culture where Buddhist, Hindu and ancient tribal religions exist side by side and often intertwine. She treats (heals) many patients every morning at her house. Patients come to visit her from around the country, as well as from India and Tibet. She sees the poorest of the poor as well as the royal family of Nepal. We were all very much looking forward to meeting this remarkable woman.

*Aama's healing room in her home in Bouddhanath*
*(Taken by Mujiba Cabugos)*

Aama's first-floor healing room is cool and inviting. It is perhaps 15' x 20' and allows patients who are waiting, space to sit on floor pillows. There is a cabinet style altar with candles and incense burning. Sacred Thangkas of Hindu deities hung on the wall along with a funky clock that lights up on the hour as electronic birds sing. Aama sat crossed-legged in her ritual chair, which was upholstered in pink floral fabric. Larry had told us that whenever she sits in this chair she is in her power. In front of the chair is a low table with a large platter of rice. Aama would sprinkle rice in the direction of the patient to make the spirits surrounding them take notice. It is also into this pile of rice that people stuck cash offerings. There were other tools of her trade on this table and the table to her right.

Larry had told us that Aama's father had been a great village shaman who had seven wives and many children. Aama and her brothers and sisters observed their father's healing rituals and would re-enact them at play. Aama would become Kali, the ferocious destructive countenance of Shiva. But girls were not supposed to become shamans, so her father refused to train her, even though she showed a particularly strong interest and aptitude. Eventually Aama dropped the notion of becoming a shaman. Then one day her family came across fortunetellers in a park in Kathmandu and she was told that someday she would be a great shaman, but not until her father died. Aama married a man named Buddha and led the normal life of a young Hindu wife. Then, when she was 27, her father died. After he had crossed over he came to Aama and become her teacher. She began to shake and her family was very worried thinking she was possessed, but it became apparent that it was her father coming into her with knowledge. Her father gave her the ability to spot sorcerers by her sense of smell. This became a problem for Aama's husband because he was in the Nepali army and Aama thought the major's wife smelled bad and Aama became very violent with her. One Christmas Aama and Buddha came home and while she was there she began to shake. Her brothers were concerned about who possessed her so they brought a lama to observe her. The voice from Aama's throat stated that he was her father. The lama tested him by saying, if that is so bring me your drum. Aama fetched it forthwith. There were other tests and the lama told the family that he was convinced that Aama's father was in her and that she was, indeed, a shaman. Her reputation grew. Eventually the Chinea Lama at the time (father of the current Chinea Lama) became ill and came to Aama in her remote village. She said he would not die and she was right. He lived to be over 90. When he was 93 or 94 he became sick again and Aama had a vision as to when he would die, but she refused to tell him. She did however alert a family member and all of his affairs were put in order and people who needed to be present were summoned. The family was so grateful that they provided her with land (when there were still fields in that part of Kathmandu) and a house and brought her to Kathmandu where she could be the most effective. The family dynamic changed at that time and her husband, Buddha, began to drink. At the time of our visit Buddha was hospitalized with cancer of the tongue.

    When we arrived, Aama was sitting in her ritual chair. She is a compact middle-aged woman with a big smile and no-nonsense eyes. She doesn't speak English, so our interpreters related what was happening.

    When we arrived a Nepali woman was sitting cross-legged in from of Aama. Her question was whether she should sell her land, how long it would take to sell and how much she should expect to be paid for it. As we were about to see

Nepalis come to a shaman for answers, derived through divination, as well as physical and spiritual healing.

*Aama counting on her fingers*
(Taken by Mujiba Cabugos)

Aama listened carefully and then began her mantra, counting on her fingers and waiting to be enlightened. Aama invokes the assistance of an army of spirit helpers including her father, tiger, monkey and some strange old Tibetan who is always asking for cigarettes and alcohol. Aama was able to answer the woman's questions and the woman bowed, tucked some folding money into the pile of rice and left.

Next came a mother with a baby. The baby was running a fever. Aama poured holy water into a crockery cup and began to stir it with her specially forged iron knife as she toned her mantra over the cup. The mother held the baby's mouth open as Aama poured the medicine in. Aama advised the woman to bring the baby back the next day.

Next came a 10-year-old girl who was sick and a woman with menstrual problems.

A woman arrived well dressed and with an upper class aura about her. Her 12-year-old niece accompanied her. The lady was from Calcutta and had come to visit her sister in Kathmandu. She discovered that her sister's husband had another woman (Ram interpreted it "another wife"). The sister had several children and the husband was no longer sleeping at home or interacting with the family. The young girl with the Calcutta lady was his daughter. He did, however, drop by on occasion. The Calcutta sister felt that the other woman had worked sorcery on him since she was older and had a baby of her own. Aama listened attentively and began her mantra and finger counting, rocking slightly as she conferred with her spirit helpers. Suddenly Aama came back from her trance state and asked the Calcutta sister, "Does this man drink [alcohol]?" The sister confirmed that he did. Aama then took a pint bottle of whiskey and poured a small amount into her potion cup, stirring it with her iron knife and toning mantras into it. She then poured the sampling of alcohol back into the pint and tipped it up to mix it thoroughly. Aama then gave the bottle to the woman and told her to offer it to the man the next time he came home. The mantras were designed to undo the sorcery of the other woman. In effect it was an Anti-Love-Potion. Aama told her to come the next day and bring another pint of alcohol and a piece of the man's clothing. What was interesting to us was that people sitting in the ritual room would ask the woman questions and the entire exercise was very public and open.

The last patient of the morning was a petite Nepali woman in her twenties dressed in a beautiful red sari. I had watched her enter as she sat near a wall, leaning against it as if she had no strength. She sat before Aama and they exchanged conversation. Ram relayed to us that a spirit possessed the woman. We had hoped to witness a depossession ceremony (a "man chinni") while in Nepal and it looked like this might be the opportunity we had hoped for. Aama began by addressing the spirit. The woman began to shake. The spirit told Aama it was a deity. Aama raised her voice and commanded that the spirit reveal its identity. Deities did not behave in such a manner! The woman shook alarmingly and her neatly pinned back hair came loose and flailed about her shoulders. Ram was interpreting for us all the while. Aama then created a circle in the air with her iron knife over the woman's head and shoulders, sealing in the spirit. The spirit was trying to escape and Aama continued to address it. "WHO ARE YOU AND WHY HAVE YOU "SPOILED" THIS WOMAN?" she shouted (in Nepali). Eventually the spirit spoke in a faint almost inaudible whisper. It seemed that the spirit was put into the woman by a female relative who was jealous of her and that the possession was also causing the woman not to become pregnant. Now having identified the spirit, Aama banished the spirit to "the crossroads" where it was deposited and left to its fate. Aama then instructed the woman to wait until the fourth day after the end of her bleeding (menstrual cycle) and at that time she would be able to conceive a child. As the woman stood up she was a little shaky, but definitely stronger and clearer. Her hair still hung loose and she was covered with sweat, but she smiled for the first time and it was very clear why another woman might be jealous of her classic beauty.

Aama then visited with us for a few minutes, warmly welcoming us and sizing up the new Dr. Larry group.

After our introduction to Aama we walked to the Bouddhanath Stupa. The streets and alleyways we traversed were dusty and we had to watch our step to keep from tripping on uneven cobblestones, sleeping dogs, and pieces of trash. I could see why wearing sandals might be a bad idea. It was conceivable that you might end up with something sharp or squishy between your toes. Larry's long-legged gait was sometimes hard to keep up with, but I figured that picking up my own gait was a good calorie burner.

*Bouddhanath Stupa*
*(Taken by Sue Melanson)*

The Bouddhanath Stupa is a key pilgrimage site for Tibetan Buddhists many of whom settled in Bouddhanath when they fled Tibet in the 1950s. A stupa is a dome-shaped reliquary structure symbolic in form. The stupa embodies the essential elements, each of its five levels representing a color, shape, element, and direction, as well as a chakra energy. The dome-shaped monument is worshipped by circumambulation…walking in a meditative state in a clockwise direction around the structure. The Bouddhanath Stupa is about the size of a football field and is the largest stupa in Nepal in terms of the amount of space it occupies. The stupa stands over a white stucco three-tiered platform. The square base of the stupa, the foundation, represents the earth element. Next is the round bulbous dome in which the Lotus symbolically resides. This represents water. Then comes an upward facing triangle or spire, symbolizing fire and scored with thirteen rings representing the steps to enlightenment. The umbrella shape represents air and the pinnacle symbolizes ether. Looking out from all four directions are the all-seeing eyes of Buddha and the Nepali numeral "one". Over 140 prayer wheels are mounted in niches surround the bottom level.

*Prayer Wheels*
*(Taken by Sue Melanson)*

A prayer wheel is a drum shaped canister in which a mantra (meditative prayer) has been written on paper over and over and inserted. On the exterior of the canister the mantra "Om Mani Padme Hum" is carved or cast. Simply touching the prayer wheel will bring purification. During meditation one spins the prayer wheel clockwise with a wrist movement. The prayer wheels surrounding the stupa are about twelve inches tall, but there were other prayer wheels in shrines around the stupa that stood four feet tall. According to legend, spinning the wheel one revolution will evoke fifty blessings.

We stopped inside the gate and paid an entry fee of 100 rupees to the Ministry of Culture, Tourism and Civil Aviation. We never paid the fee again, so I have to assume it was a voluntary contribution. The stupa is massive and since it is completely surrounded by buildings you don't see it until you are standing directly in front of it. Private homes, monasteries, shops and street vendors surround the structure. Jigme shared with us that no one pees near the stupa "for fear they will have problems with their pee pee place". Those deities can be a wrathful bunch!

Legend has it that in the 7th century a very pious Buddhist woman came into possession of a bone fragment that belonged to the Buddha. Wanting to honor and preserve this precious relic, she asked the King of Nepal for permission to build a stupa to house the artifact. The king agreed to the construction but with the restriction that the footprint of the stupa be limited to the size of one water buffalo skin. The woman agreed and then purchased the largest hide she could find. She cut it into thin strips then sewed them together end to end to form the perimeter. The king had no choice but to allow her this space for the massive structure.

We began by circumambulating the stupa, spinning the prayer wheels as we walked. After we completed our circumambulation Erica handed around a container of Purell (an antibiotic hand washing gel), which was probably an excellent idea. It just would not have been couth to spin the prayer wheels wearing latex gloves!

We then climbed the steep steps to the second level of the stupa base. To my surprise the surface was not flat but had a rolling terrain, and I had to watch my step. From our new vantage point we could see the activity in the marketplace surrounding the stupa. Nearby, a couple of Buddhist priests were making amulets. They would first fold a piece of paper with prayers and meditations written on it into a tight packet about an inch square. Then they would carefully weave strings of various colors around the prayers, creating an attractive pattern.

*Buddhist Prayer Amulet*
(Taken by Sue Melanson)

Some were encased in plastic and others were not, and each was priced accordingly. At Larry's suggestion, each of us bought one to afford us protection while on our journey, Sano Ram blessed them and tied them around our necks.

We meandered through the vendors and praying faithful around the stupa and stopped near the Bouddha Ghyang, a shrine housing ornate statues of the five Dhyani Meditation Buddhas. Vairochana and his lion were at the center representing "consciousness". Next came Achhyobhya in the east and his elephant. He represents "form". Ratnasambhava is in the south on his horse representing "feeling". Amitabh is in the west on his peacock representing "perception". And Amoghasiddi is in the north on his garuda (bird-man) representing "volition". In front of the deities are butter lamps made from ghee, clarified yak butter, that one can pay to light helping departed loved ones on their journey.

I lit one for Don Chaffee, my life-long friend who died of lung cancer last October at age 59. And just to give them some backup, I lit one for my mother and one for Marlene Reading's mother. They are both getting near the end of this lifetime's journey.

Beside the stupa is a two-story pagoda style temple to the Hindu goddess Ajima. Ajima is the goddess of smallpox and she is depicted eating the intestines of a child she has stretched across her lap. Buddha was alarmed by the smallpox epidemic, controlled by the goddess, and decided to teach her a lesson in compassion. Ajima had thousands of children, it is said, but her favorite was her youngest. Buddha chose that child and hid it under a basket. Ajima was frantic trying to find her youngest child. Finally she came to Buddha and asked, "What have you done with my child?" Buddha explained that he wanted her to feel the suffering of other mothers who lost their children to the smallpox plague. He then returned the child to Ajima and Ajima's heart was softened and she felt compassion and ended the plague.

We poked into a few shops, making note of the ones we hoped to explore later.

Suju's bus was waiting for us and we decided to make a stop at the Gemini Market, which is part grocery store, part pharmacy and part sundries shop. I was in need of a clock, shoelaces for my sneakers, a battery for my watch, nail clippers and bottled water. Instead I picked up some elegant bubble bath, a bar of basil/parsley glycerin soap and a Toblerone chocolate bar.

Jigme stayed close to us explaining what some items were. He also introduced us to Yarchagumba Tea, which is purported to be good for sex and for arthritis. The Baby Boomers dream! Jigme was very animated as he explained that the tea is made from a grass that grows high in the Himalayas and is a grass for 6 months and an insect for 6 months. That possibility seemed highly unlikely, so I looked it up on-line and discovered that it was actually a fungus that ingests insects. Despite my skepticism about its medicinal and aphrodisiac properties, I bought two boxes. After all, what if Jigme was RIGHT?

We had a late leisurely lunch on the balcony of a local restaurant. So leisurely, it took forty-five minutes to create a veggie burger for Larry and Jeff. I was thirsty, so I went for a Sweet Lassie, a big bottle of water and shared a plate of fried potatoes with Denise.

In the afternoon it was difficult for Suju to get the bus right to our doorstep at the hotel. I never figured out why, but assume it had to do with traffic patterns. So we had several blocks to walk on our way "home". Our route took us past Shaym Pandit's tee shirt shop, which had been highly recommended by both Pramod and Dr. Larry. Over the course of our stay we all dropped a fair number of rupees with Shaym.

Back at the Tibet Guest House we were becoming better acclimated and set about arranging more nitty gritty details of everyday life, like obtaining safe deposit boxes and changing money at the front desk.

We were all tired, dusty and hot, but pleased with how much we had experienced in one day. The rest of the trip promised extraordinary things if we kept up the same pace.

I wasn't much interested in dinner, but eventually succumbed and sat in the restaurant garden with Denise and had a bowl of cream of mushroom soup which tasted surprisingly like Campbell's.

April 1$^{st}$ was not only April Fool's Day but also the birthday of TWO of our band of travelers. Sarah turned 61 and Denise turned 49, so Larry ordered a cake and we had a small celebration in the dining room. There isn't a lot of sugar in the Nepali diet; hence the cake gave most of us a sugar zing just in time for bed.

Sarah was handing out Ambian to those of us who were having trouble sleeping, but a sugar neutralizer, if there is such a thing, may have worked better.

# CHAPTER 8
## April 2, 2006 SUNDAY
## PASHUPATI, MOMOS AND PICKLE, AND THANGKAS

When I was growing up, especially during the years of teenage heartbreak and drama, Daddy used to tell me that people who are able to open their hearts and live and love deeply and sincerely have something that people who live isolated and suspicious lives don't. They have "shoeboxes". Daddy would try to comfort his ailing (and wailing) daughters by telling us to pack up all our emotional heartache into a mental shoebox and tuck it high on a back shelf in our memory. Then, someday when it didn't hurt so much, you can take down the shoebox and examine the contents and realize how special the relationship, friendship or love was. Today is April 2 and I have two shoeboxes that are having birthdays. John is a college beau who earned a shoebox way back then and later played an encore...that shoebox is still a little too prickly to look at. It has to "age" some more. The other is James, my stepson. His shoebox came about when he decided to severe connections with his father and I. I still don't understand it, but after all the years that have elapsed I have to acknowledge that we are estranged. Nevertheless, a happy birthday wish went out into the ether to both of them.

The food here tends to be very spicy and curry is in everything, so I have been seeking out the blander offerings. Erica ordered an Indian Breakfast that reeked of spice while I ordered Muesli and Fruit in Curd -- just like Miss Muffet who sat on her tuffet. The order arrived in a tiny little bowl, but it was rich and stuck to my ribs.

Nepal has been having a drought. The country is hydro-powered, so lack of water is a big problem. Every morning there is a power blackout to save electricity. This is also the reason you don't find ice cream in Nepal. The outages are just long enough to cause meltdowns. There is, however, one restaurant called Fire and Ice that has an ice cream freezer generator. They are the only place in the city of Kathmandu with ice cream.

Our morning began, as it did yesterday, with a visit to the Ganesh Shrine to ask for his blessing as we began our day, and then we boarded Suju's bus and went on to Aama's healing room.

Larry had told us that not all shamans use the same techniques Aama does.

He had told us about Lhamo who has died. She would embody a fierce Tara, which is the female consort of a Buddha. When she was a young girl she gave all her worldly goods to the poor and went in search of a teacher whom she eventually found and who taught her the extraction techniques she used in her healings. A lot of her extraction practices were quite violent, during which she would pounce on the patient and bite them, or suck poisonous substances out of them with a copper tube. Some patients claim they had to go to another shaman to be healed of the wounds inflicted by the spirits working through Lhamo. Lhamo would extract what ailed her patients in non-ordinary reality and then manifest whatever she found in ordinary reality. She typically removed blood, pus and pieces of meat from the patient. Traditionally shamans eat what they extract to neutralize them. This was impossible for Lhamo since she would often have a whole table full of disgusting extraction materials when she was through, and she had to use other methods to destroy the foul collection. Larry told us about a patient he had witnessed who arrived at Lhamo's walking, literally, on the edges of her misshapen feet. Lhamo quickly divined that a spirit was causing the woman's torment. Lhamo yelled at the spirit, bartered with the spirit and stuck the sharp end of a phurba (a wooden three-faced ritual dagger) into the soles of the woman's feet. The woman -- or rather the spirit – howled in pain and begged her to stop. Before long the spirit realized it had met its match and promised not to "spoil" the woman again. Larry said that the woman's feet straightened out and she never had an episode again. Lhamo's fame spread and eventually she was asked to visit Russia and Sweden. She was strongly advised not to go, as it was foreseen that the trip would affect her health. She went anyway. When she returned to Nepal she had a kidney attack and died.

Maya was Aama's sister and they worked closely together, often doing a "good cop/bad cop" routine with invasive spirits. Maya could conjure up unbelievable threats against the bad spirits.

The last time Larry brought a group to Nepal, Maya had been suffering from cancer of the spine. Just before the Full Moon Initiation, Maya came out of her house and hung a mala of flowers around his neck, then, silently, returned to her house. During the Initiation, Larry says that he never danced so hard. He danced for Maya's healing, but she died two months before we arrived. Larry was grieving.

On our way to Aama's on this particular day, we had the opportunity to ask questions.

One of our group was curious about the iron knife Aama uses in her healings. Larry explained that the knife is forged by a blacksmith (also considered a healer) and cannot be machine made. The iron in the forged knife has power over death.

Another question was about the possessed woman who had been there the first day. What exactly possessed her?

Larry explained that there is a difference between natural illnesses that arise on their own, and illnesses caused by possession. There are two types of possession, one by eternal beings (deities and demons) and the other by harmful spirits of the dead called "laagu" or graveyard ghosts. Deities or demons take over the earthly body of a person to accomplish a mission. If the possessing entity is a deity and the mission is a worthy one, the possession could be considered an honor. If the possession is by a demon, it's not good! It is possible for a graveyard ghost to attack a person on its own, but it is more common that it would be under the control of a "boksha" (male) or a "bokshi" (female). In Western terminology a boksha/bokshi is a witch or sorcerer/sorceress. The type of laagu is determined by the circumstances of their demise, but they generally have met an unnatural death or were not afforded a proper funeral. One type of laagu called a "masaan" is a graveyard ghost consisting of a whisp of the soul of a dead person that didn't make it into the life beyond. They usually are not evil, but are simply lost and cannot find their way. They hang around, have human emotions, and get upset and frustrated that they can't move on. They can cause illness that is often indicative of the manner in which they died. These Illnesses are of a consumptive nature, as if the afflicted one is being eaten. By offering "food" (whatever the hungry masaan craves) a shaman can barter with the masaan and move it on to where it needs to be for the higher good of all. Sorcerers are masters of deceit and may capture a hungry ghost by feeding it. Then they can control it and cause it to "spoil" its victims, as we saw in the case of the woman in the red sari.

Larry was asked what the difference is between a shaman and a lama. A shaman does healings and is concerned with everyone, good and bad, living and dead. A lama is concerned only with the "good" and teaches esoteric values while people are alive, helping them towards goodness and the light. Lamas perform death ceremonies and assist the soul, but they don't work with the bad, the dark or the evil.

During our second day in Aama's healing room, the Calcutta lady with the wandering brother-in-law returned. She reported that her sister's husband had come to the house the evening before and he had imbibed the whiskey with the anti-love-spell in it. The Calcutta lady had brought a second bottle of whisky for Aama to treat. Aama toned her mantra over the bottle and told the woman to repeat the libation.

A willowy blond Westerner came before Aama. She was married to an exiled member of the royal family. She wanted to know if it was safe for her husband, who was not in Nepal, to return. Aama told her that he could come for a brief visit in October but that it was unsafe for him to stay.

There is a saying that we are beginning to hear quite a bit, which in Nepali means "You're having a run of bad luck." They call it "din dasa graha" - bad days and planets.

Today was the first time one of us sat before Aama for healing. I was the first one. I had thought about what I would ask late into the night (before the Ambian neutralized the birthday cake sugar). Perhaps I intellectualized what I was asking too much, but this is what I came up with.

I want to walk in this life more effectively.
My body feels tired and aches.
I feel cluttered and want to feel clear.
I have questions:
Am I living in the place I should be?
Am I doing what I should be?
How can I make my life more meaningful?

I wrote out my request and handed it to Ram so he could figure out how best to interpret for me. He also said that I should speak my request to Aama. He had some difficulty coming up with a meaningful word for "cluttered". We agreed on "scattered and crowded".

My knees bother me and I cannot sit cross-legged on the floor. Part of it is that I am not used to it, part of it is the fact that I ripped my left knee when I fell in our kennel six years ago, and part of it is arthritis. Aama provided a low stool for me so I would not have to sit on the floor. I sat in front of Aama and quietly repeated my question. I could feel the incense that was burning on her altar enveloping me like a cloud, although I knew it was not physically happening. She looked at my knees and tapped them. Then she began her mantra divination exercise, which begins: "Shep Se Te Nee..." While she did her thing I was observing the things she had on her table besides the platter of rice. There was the iron knife with the antler or bone handle. There was a small bronze chalice of holy ash. She had a pitcher of water and a jar of a dark liquid that I later learned was mustard oil. She had a broom that she would use to beat bad spirits out of a patient. I stopped being so analytical and tried to concentrate on what she was doing. Ram was explaining something to the group, but I wasn't following what he was saying. The funky bird clock chimed the hour. I felt like I was inside a bubble in a very chaotic world. Finally, Aama spoke to me (through Ram). She said I should bring a small container the next day and she would put a mantra into some mustard oil for me to rub on my knees. She also said that my problems were physical, not spiritual. In other words, there was no spirit or sorcerer causing me problems. She said that whatever I undertook, I would be successful in whatever place I chose to live. She advised me to obtain an image of the Singh Devi (Durga) and set it in the east facing the west. I should then sit facing the east and make a practice of meditating in front of it. I was a little disappointed. I expected something more dramatic. Aama threw rice on me, touched the top of my head and I was dismissed. I took my stool to the back of the room and sat down while others came before Aama.

Aama had invited us to lunch and we gathered in her upstairs room to wait. Each of us had brought what was termed a "spirit gift" with us from our homes. Erica had a little box woven from Arizona pine needles. I had brought a tiny silver turtle pin that was embellished with coral and turquoise. Since the turtle represents so much to the Native Americans I figured it would be a good "spirit gift". It was given to me by another shaman and to her from yet another, so it has an interesting history of owners. I was very pleased with my choice, but the interpreters were having trouble telling Aama that it was a turtle. Finally Pramod told her it was a Sari Pin. I had the feeling that the special nature of my gift had been, quite literally, lost in translation.

Lunch was momos, pancake like breads that are called rotis, fried potatoes and plates of watermelon and papaya pieces. It was a delightful meal, sitting in the breeze by the window in Aama's upstairs living room.

After we left Aama's we walked to Pashupatinath. Along the way we passed carefully irrigated fields and small farmyards with one or two cows. We came upon a vacant lot of self-seeded greenery and Pramod took the opportunity to test Burt's knowledge of plant life. Pramod asked him, "Do you know what this is?" Burt came over, looked closely at the foliage, sniffed it, turned it over in his hand and told Pramod that it must be a member of a particular Latin genus plant family. Pramod laughed and said simply, "It's grass!" And so it was: "cannabis sativa, otherwise known as hemp, cannabis, marijuana or GRASS.

Pashupati is the most important Hindu temple complex in Nepal.

To begin with we needed a little background on the Hindu trinity. Brahma is the creator. Vishu is the preserver. Śhiva is the destroyer and, even though he represents destruction, he is viewed as a positive force. Without destruction and death the universe would be choked with life because there would be no exit strategy.

We paid our 250 rupees ($3.50 US) at the gatehouse and ascended an ancient staircase to the left of the main courtyard, which is only accessible to Hindus (or, more accurately, Asian looking people). Aama entered the main courtyard and brought out tika for all of us.

We began a long climb up broad stone stairs with small stupas and shrines on either side. Ancient trees gave shade to the stairs and monkeys roam freely in the protected temple grounds.

*Monkey on the stone stairs*
(Taken by Mujiba Cabugos)

This stairway is referenced in Led Zeppelin's "Stairway to Heaven".

*There's a feeling I get when I look to the west*
*And my spirit is crying for leaving*
*In my thoughts I have seen rings of smoke through the trees*
*And the voices of those who stand looking.*

The long climb took us through what had been the Slesmantak Forest in ancient times. It is said that Lord Shiva, living the perfect life of a deity in his glittering palace at Mount Kailash, decided to duck out on his responsibilities, and even his beautiful wife, Parvati. It was to this forest that Shiva came, taking the form of a one-horned stag and calling himself Pashupati, the Lord of Animals. He romped in this forest for several hundred years until other gods discovered who he was and came to fetch him. They broke off his horn and it became the shivalingam that is worshipped here. Legend says that Shiva called Brahma and Vishnu to honor the lingam and he challenged them to locate its end. Vishnu mounted his Garuda vehicle and journeyed downward, but he could not find the end of the lingam. He realized that there was no end, so he came back and said to Shiva, "There is no end." Meanwhile, Brahma, on his swan, journeyed upward to heaven looking for the end of the lingam. Likewise he could not find the end but he picked a flower and brought it back to Shiva. He told Shiva that he had found the end of the lingam and he had picked a flower from the spot to prove where he was. He then told Shiva, "If you don't believe me, ask the cow. She will tell you." But Brahma had brainwashed the cow, so when Shiva asked the cow, "Is this true?" The cow's head said "Yes" (vertical nodding) but her tail said "No" (horizontal swaying). And so it remains today. A cow walking will nod her head "yes" but her tail is always saying "No".

*Shivalingam shrine at Pashupati*
*(Taken by Sue Melanson)*

The shivalingam we saw in one of the shrines has obvious phallic symbolism but also denotes the primeval energy of Shiva. The lingam is mounted on a circular receptacle, which provides the practical function of draining off water offered during ablution ceremonies, but also represents the female yoni and sexual energy.

But back to our story.

Restless as he was, Lord Shiva once more escaped from Kailash and came back to the forest as a hunter. This time his wife, Parvati, followed him and disguised herself as a beautiful huntress. Shiva tried to seduce her, and discovering her true identity returned home to Mount Kailash in shame. The Kirateswar Temple commemorates Shiva's vacation-gone-bad.

*Sadhu at Pashupati.*
*I had to pay the sadhu 40 rupees to take his photo.*
(Taken by Sue Melanson)

In addition to the aggressive monkeys, there are some scary looking sadhus wandering the Pashupati environs. They are holy men, covered in ashes, with long beads, dreadlocks, and wearing loincloths. They have given up all their worldly goods to follow a spiritual path and Shiva cares for them. According to Hindu tradition, sadhus don't get cremated because they have already left this world, they will be buried.

The Gujeshwari temple commemorates the story of Lord Shiva's first love, Sati. Shiva and Sati had been married, but Sati's father was not happy with her choice of husbands and considered Shiva to be an ash-covered sadhu. Sati, however, was quite happy with the match and the two lived happily together. Then word came that Sati's father was preparing a huge feast and he had invited all Sati's sisters and their mates, but he did not invite Sati and Shiva. Sati was insulted and stated to Shiva that a daughter does not need an invitation to visit her father. So she went anyway. She arrived and discovered that her father had intentionally set out to humiliate Shiva by not inviting him. Sati became so angry that she threw herself onto the fire (some versions say she died of spontaneous combustion), but in any case, she died. Shiva was grief stricken at the death of Sati and he began to wander in the three nether worlds carrying the dead body of Sati in his arms. So violent was his stride that the universe began to tremble and there was suffering everywhere. Vishnu stepped in at this point in order to save the universe. There are two stories. The first story indicates that Vishnu shot some arrows from his bow and cut the corpse of Sati into fifty-one pieces and the pieces fell in fifty-one different parts of the country where they are worshipped as Shakti Pithas. The other story says that Vishnu invented bacteria and decay in order to decompose the body of Sati, and as Shiva ran hither and yon carrying her body, parts began to drop off and the Shakti Pithas are the places where her parts fell. Either way, you have a dismemberment legend.

    I found myself becoming disoriented and anxious as we walked amongst the temples and shrines along the staircase. I stuck close to the group, but the group seemed to be moving off in different directions. I didn't really feel afraid of anything; I was just very uncomfortable. I was also very hot and perhaps dehydrated. Erica and Susan were busy capturing every detail on film. I became concerned that Erica was not keeping track of her pocketbook as she maneuvered to take artistic shots with her camera. An intense Nepali boy had been watching us and began to follow as we moved around. He was making me nervous. I pointed him out to Erica and she immediately began to heed the whereabouts of her pocketbook. The Dr. Larry group seemed to be splintering into different groups. That also made me anxious. Susan had drifted off with Aama and Mujiba was sitting on the steep steps opposite the ghats watching a cremation in progress. Erica and I joined Mujiba and sat on the steps, keenly aware that the strange boy had perched close by.

    It is believed that to die and be cremated here will release one from the cycle of repeated birth and death. The large white buildings across the river are what could be termed a hospice. The Hindi faithful bring their dying family members here to pass their final weeks, days or hours in the holy place and their families care them for. Even royalty comes here. Once someone has passed from this life their cremation can take place quickly in the holiest of sites in Nepal.

I was not unfamiliar with the Hindu cremation concept or the ghats, but seeing them in person was a different experience. The ghats are stone slabs that jut out over the river. Families bring their dead and ritually prepare the bodies for cremation. The saffron color death shroud is soaked in combustible oil and a candle is secured in the mouth of the deceased. The sons light the candle, and as it burns down it eventually lights the funeral pyre. Family members grieve in cloistered areas just behind the ghats, tending the fire until the cremation is complete. The ashes of the deceased are then swept into the Bagmati River, which is a tributary of the Ganges, and the process is complete. The ghats in front of the Shiva Temple are reserved for royalty. Women used to throw themselves on their husband's funeral pyre to be burned alive, but that practice, called "sati", has been outlawed in Nepal.

*Funeral pyre on a ghat at Pashupati*
*(Taken by Mujiba Cabugos)*

The cremation across the way had been going on for many hours and the funeral pyre was smoldering down to a heap of ash. Because of the drought the Bagmati River was not flowing as it should. In fact it wasn't flowing at all. What was left of the water was a wet area about twelve feet across bordered by a wide riverbank that should have been under water. Pickers roamed the riverbank looking for unburned pieces of wood for their own fuel, or human remains that could be sold on the black market. Trumpets made from human thighbones are considered holy relics, and skulls are also desirable. Jigme pointed out that the pickers were also looking for gold teeth. I sat and watched and snapped a few discreet photos to be added to my "You just won't believe this one" page. The strange boy continued to stare at us with an unnerving, unblinking gaze. Another group of people appeared to be bathing in the stagnant Bagmati River waters, but I soon realized that they were actually bathing another dead body. After his final holy bath, they wrapped him (yes, it was definitely a "him") in a yellow shroud and four men carried the body to a pyre that was not yet lit. I was relieved when Larry suggested we move along. The steps were suddenly very very steep and I was experiencing a touch of vertigo. The sun was very hot and that strange boy was relentlessly staring. Erica had shielded her face to avoid his stare. I was also anticipating the imminent lighting of funeral pyre number two, and the combination of the smells of burning wood, burning oil-soaked cloth and burning flesh wasn't appealing.

We crossed the river and stopped to look at a shivalingam shrine. One of our group commented on how peaceful and serene the place was even with all the people and the hustle and bustle. I did not get that serenity hit at all. Pashupatinath was weirding me out!

A large tent had been set up behind the temples and shrines and a crowd was participating in some kind of holy event.

We headed for a row of shops along the street where we could buy ochre powder in a variety of colors, crystal malas, bronze statues and singing bowls. While the shoppers amongst us bartered for their wares, the rest of us waited near the shop entrance.

A band of young urchins began inching up to Denise and whacking her derriere, then fleeing into the crowd before anyone could react. Larry became her bodyguard and stationed himself between Denise and the youthful assailants.

Meanwhile I began a conversation with Gauri that compounded my increasing queasiness. I was determined to find a Durga statue to take home with me in compliance with Aama's instructions. I asked Gauri to help me find one. He seized the opportunity to tell me about the wonderful Durga Thangka that he had in his shop, and the idea sounded good to me. After all, carrying a rolled up scroll home with me sounded preferable to a solid bronze statue, no matter how small.

We headed off to meet Suju's bus that was waiting for us in a parking lot nearby. I was afraid we were going to have to climb up and over the steep steps of the hillock through the forest again, but we didn't. On the way to the bus an army of street vendors besieged us. Larry had taught us a very useful Nepali phrase, "Chain dayna" which means "Don't need any." The vendors followed us right up to the bus and pounded on the windows to get our attention. I think I knew in that moment what the definition of "pandemonium" is. I was living it!

Once again, the bus could not make it to the Tibet Guest House and we were obliged to walk the extra blocks. Sarah, Susan and Mujiba stopped in a shop and asked Ram to barter for them. I stopped with them and was soon regretting my decision. The rest of the group had headed for "home" and I was quite turned around and disoriented. I had no idea which way "home" was, so I had to stay with the shoppers.

Susan was interested in personal prayer wheels on handles. Mujiba had lost an eye to a set of jade offering bowls, and Sarah was admiring a necklace made of chunky silver beads. I recognized the Meditation Tara ritual masks Larry had used in one of our workshops. Had I not been so overdone, I might have also become a shopper.

By the time we got back to the Tibet Guest House I was a little dizzy and nauseous. I hoped the cure would be a cool shower, a dose of Imodium with an Ibuprofen chaser, and a long long drink of water. I sat alone to realign my senses. I could have taken a nap, but I chose to journey.

*JOURNEY:*
My main power animal is the Horseshoe Crab. He has ancient wisdom, has remained genetically unaltered through the ages and provides me with a strong shield of armor. There

are also magical properties in his blue-colored blood that will coagulate in the presence of certain types of bacteria and viruses as a warning. We often travel together at great rates of speed underwater or through the heavens. Sometimes I ride his back and sometimes I become a passenger inside his thick shell. Today I was on his back with the wind in my hair soaring high up in the Himalayas. We circled the mountain peaks and I could feel the contrast of the hot sun above and the cold snow below. Contrasts, hot and cold, dark and light, good and bad. The message I was being given was that there are ancestors in the mountains...no, the mountains ARE the ancestors...and they hold secrets of power and protection for me. The Horseshoe Crab lowered me into a cave and left me standing in the dark, blinking and trying to adjust to the dimness after soaring in the blinding snow-light. I became aware of teeny specks of light that looked like fiber optics that glowed blue/green in the stone chamber. Intuitively I knew this to be the Himalayan retreat of my yi-dam. I turned and my yi-dam stood in an arched doorway. Behind him appeared to be some palatial palace or cathedral. He stepped forward into the chamber and suddenly wicker chairs appeared for us to sit in. He offered me a Swiss Almond Mocha ice cream sundae but I felt uncomfortable eating alone. My yi-dam explained that they no longer make his favorite flavor, so he accepted my offer to share. We sat in the glowing chamber, eating ice cream and being silent in each other's company. As we neared the bottom of the crystal ice cream parlor glass, he stopped and took my hand in his. He laid a spoonful of chilly ice cream on my palm and told me to eat it. It was sticky but I licked it clean. He took my hand a second time and placed a spoonful of mocha almond on the back of my hand. This was harder to eat, but I managed. His eyes became very intense, as they do whenever he has a lesson for me. His body also emanates the scent of lavender whenever he is ready to teach me. "Do you know why you are here? Why you have come to this place?" I was confused. Did he mean to this non-ordinary reality cave, or to Nepal? He read my confusion and explained that I was not in the Kathmandu Valley by accident. "The plan for you is far greater than a simple $60^{th}$ birthday present trip-of-a-lifetime from your devoted husband. Your initiation into the discipline, the power and the energy of being a shaman will be completed here."

On the April full moon it will have been 54 months (half of the sacred 108 number) since my first initiation and transfer of knowledge. I was now seasoned enough to be asked again. My answers would be governed not only by my gut response, but also by the maturity of my experience. And this initiation would contain – must contain – an element of physical exertion. I will be asked again, three times, "Do you agree? Are you capable? Are you strong enough, powerful enough? Do you believe?" And from this Himalayan power place I will take into every fiber of my being the power, the energy, the discipline and healing ability not only for others but for myself and for the world. And I will not be standing alone. There are others like me everywhere. The isolation of doing "the work" will be less. Shamanic practice is reaching critical mass. But for me, personally, this journey is still a work in progress. I must complete my assignment. My yi-dam then removed his tall blue green and gilt headpiece and laid it on a ledge that appeared to be an altar. It seemed like he had removed the hair, skin and cranial bone of his head with the headpiece and the crown of his head shone brilliantly in the cave. He read the surprise in my eyes and explained that this is the way he opens his crown chakra. It was dramatic! A little cushion, something like a flying carpet, dropped from the ceiling and hovered in front of me. He motioned me to sit on it. It was lotus shaped. It rose up and darted through the ether.

I was suddenly back in Room 304 at the Tibet Guest House in Kathmandu.

By the time we gathered to walk to Gauri's thangka shop for dinner, I was functional, energized by my venture into non-ordinary reality but my gastro-intestinal tract was certainly not up to par.

Thangkas are Nepalese paintings of religious themes. The good ones are intricately detailed and painted with stone ink and gold. The finished product is then mounted in a heavy brocade frame, and hung by a pole that may or may not have decorative gold or silver end knobs. A protective lightweight fabric screen can be raised or lowered over the central

Thangka to protect it from sun. Larry has a large museum-quality collection of Thangkas in his home.

*Nepalese Thangka*

Gauri was anxious to show me the Durga thangka he had told me about when we were at Pashupatinath. The piece was not yet mounted and measured about 18" x 24" and depicted Durga and her tiger "vehicle". In the foreground was a cow lying on the ground with a severed head and a lot of other symbolic images. The colors were vivid and the gilt detail gave the entire piece depth. Gauri laid it on a table and weighted down the corners so I could examine it. I walked across the room and viewed it from a distance. It was, indeed, a remarkable work of art. He explained that if I wanted it, I could come the next day and we would select the fabric for the frame and it would be ready before I left for home. I was convincing myself that I needed this piece of Nepali culture even knowing that it carried a $1,500 US price tag. I sat in front of the piece for a very long time waiting for it to "speak" to me. I was doing a very good job talking myself into the piece, and so was Gauri.

Meanwhile, the group was seated on floor pillows in Gauri's back showroom admiring the Buddhas, Taras (female consorts of the Buddhas) and Mandalas (symbolic shapes) mounted on the walls. A wide variety of his selections were rolled out on the floor for viewing and some decisions were being made to purchase. There was a very large Buddha sitting in a lotus blossom painted in rose, deep red and gold that was beautiful, and very pricey. My Durga was beginning to look like a bargain. I wished I had been able to grab my cell phone and access Art's opinion. I knew he would back up my decision, but $1,500 was a heavy ticket price and we were only in our second full day in Kathmandu.

Gauri's Thangka painters had also painted the handcrafted shaman drums (dhyangros) that we were going to use for our Shamanic Initiation. The plan was for each of us to select a drum the next day and take it across the street to a tailor who could make drum covers for us out of ornate pillow covers from India.

We were Gauri's guests for dinner. He served several family style platters of momos (steamed dumplings), fried potatoes and fried rice. As was their custom there was always that very spicy "pickle" as an accompaniment.

My stomach was still a little off kilter from my day and the momos pushed me over the edge. I paid a couple of visits to the traditional Nepali squat toilet (as opposed to Western "tall toilets") secreted behind a panel in Gauri's back showroom and, after an uncomfortably long evening during which I agreed to buy the Durga Thangka, I was glad to be back in my room.

# CHAPTER 9
## April 3, 2006 MONDAY
## SWAYAMBHU, CHILLS AND THE KURTA SHOP

Monday was Swayambhu Day, and I very much looked forward to it.

*The Swayambhu Story*

Originally, the Katmandu valley was a lake called Nagarad where the nags (serpents) lived. In Buddhist tradition nags are not slithering conniving creatures of Western mythology, but highly respected keepers of wisdom. The story goes that the Buddhist saint Manjushree Bodhisattva came from China and threw a lotus seed into the lake and it grew into a thousand petaled lotus flower from which radiated a five-colored light bringing the five Dhyani Meditation Buddhas – Vairochana, Akshobhya, Ratnasambhava, Amitabha and Amoghasiddha into the lotus. Manjushree Bodhisattva looked out over the lake wondering how he could drain the lake to allow the people to worship the lotus light and live in the beautiful valley. With his flaming sword of wisdom, he cut through the valley walls draining the lake through four gorges. He made little lakes as homes for the nags and taught the people agriculture. The lotus was then transformed into a hill and the light became the Swayambhu Stupa. The name of the place came to be Swayambhu, meaning 'Self-Created or Self-Existent', not constructed.

My introduction to Swayambhu and the Meditation Buddhas and their Taras began in May, 2004 when I was participating in a workshop with Larry, the purpose of which was to experience in journey, meditation, and masked dance, the dynamic energies of the spirit elements, directions, and lights, for personal growth, inspiration, and realization. The workshop had an initiatory structure and purpose, culminating in a "nature journey" to enlist the aid of the elemental spirits for healing. For two days we had been journeying with the help of the Meditation Buddhas and their Taras to find and heal places within ourselves that needed mending.

*JOURNEY:*
Our final journey was set forward in four parts.

1.) First, we were to create, in non-ordinary reality, a huge bumba (a vessel designed to hold soma/holy water/elixir/nectar of healing) and invite the Meditation Buddhas, Taras and other deities to pour their lights into the bumba filling it with a luminous healing liquid which we called Soma.

A great bumba had appeared as a lake in the crater of a great volcano. The volcano was, in fact, at the top of Mt. Everest, and emblazoned on the side of the mountain were "tattoos" or maps of the world. Different countries glowed red as if covered with hot lava. Prominent were Iraq, Afghanistan, North Korea, Ireland, various African and Southeast Asian countries I could not identify, Antarctica and the United States. If the volcano erupted it would send waves of soma over all these regions healing them...or wiping them out, if necessary.

I pulled back and back until I was able to see that the entire world was, in fact, the bumba. The crater at the top of Mt. Everest was simply the opening through which the bumba could be filled.

As I watched, thousands of birds or bird-like deities carried bands of fresh reeds, weaving them into a basket that enveloped the entire globe. At the top of each of the reeds delicate fairy creatures (I think they were from Atlantis) affixed crystals of all colors. This was a very active and busy image, although not one of chaos, just intense focused activity.

While the birds continued their weaving, I invited the Meditation Buddhas and their Taras to pour their lights into the bumba. I felt that this was going to be very BIG and told them so. I needed every bit of help they could offer for healing. They hovered around the rim of the crater and cried tears of Soma, healing and compassion into it. The Buddhas and their Taras then took up an observation post on their lotus thrones arranged in mandala form on what appeared to be a space ship. I then cried my own tears and discovered that my tears were actually blood. Following that, other deities from every culture came forward and also cried into the crater: Hassidic Jews, an Amish man, a representation of Wakan Tanka (Native American), various versions of Christ from various fine art images, Madonnas of all sorts, St. Bernadette, Joan of Arc, Moses, Mayans, Incas, African deities with whom I was previously unfamiliar, Egyptian deities (especially the cat god, Bas), Laurie Cabot of Wiccan fame, Greek and Roman gods and goddesses, Zeus, Thor, Nordic gods and even extra terrestrials. Vast numbers came to shed tears of healing and compassion into the crater bumba.

The bumba was full – the Whole Earth (Gaia) in fact, had a full belly of Soma. It was pregnant with Life.

2.) The second part of the journey is as follows: I was directed to invite Protectors and Witnesses -- ferocious aspects of the Buddhas and the Taras and all other guides. I explained in my invitation that this was a very big, "no fooling around" opportunity to assist in a ritual that had the potential to heal the world. I needed their help to establish order and act as Gate Keepers because we would be voluntarily inviting into our midst, in a welcoming manner, some very very Bad Boys. Amongst themselves they had to create the ultimate Geneva Convention and create it in a sacred way that was clear and concise and non-corruptible, since their charge was to keep everyone safe. Various groups of these Watchers took up posts around the world at sacred sites: Machu Picu, the Great Pyramid, Sedona, Easter Island, Stonehenge, a waterfall in Africa, and others.

It was then that the luminous waters of the bumba crater began to bubble up in a golden churning. Out of the Soma rose the Ark of the Covenant and hovered over the center of the crater at the very top of the world.

3.) I was now ready to invite all dark energies, past and present, to come forward for the banquet of Soma…for healing. My invitation list included ghosts, ghouls, skeletons, corpse eaters, those who brought/bring epidemics and plagues, and those who bring forth financial chaos. There were oil company magnets and manipulators of world oil markets, commodities dealers who trade in oil futures; King Henry VIII; Genghis Khan; Enron executives and others who were not as well known (or have yet to be discovered); politicians at all levels; religious cult leaders; get-rich-quick scheme perpetrators; scam artists; corrupt nursing home administrators and employees; unethical physicians (a lot of plastic surgeons); a lot of lawyers; scientists who were genetically altering crops and cloning animals; pimps and sexual predators of all kinds (including those who roam the internet and others who wear religious frocks); sadistic educators; Rasmussen; members of secret societies; tabloid "reporters"; Hugh Heffner and Larry Flint; Red Dog (from Lynn Andrews writing); creators of violent computer games that dull the sensibilities of young minds; Hollywood exploiters (Mel Gibson was among these folks) – the guest list was so long and varied and nasty that I could feel myself becoming faint with the disgust I was feeling. I looked to the Buddha Aksobhya, who never feels disgust, anger or hatred, and he lifted me into his lap.

Now the guests began to arrive.

Before me stood Dr. Joseph Mengela. I did not recognize his persona but I could feel his history…almost as if a documentary film was fast-forwarding through my gut. I reached deep into my heart and faced him with soul-to-soul compassion. I explained that we were preparing a grand banquet at which he would be offered the healing Soma that had been prepared. He wished to speak to me and we sat down at what seemed like a bistro table and we drank Chai together. He explained that when an entity does something that affects his/her karma so negatively that they have to come back and do a re-run of life, they return with that negativity, and short of a spiritual event or healing, they usually live their next go-round doing even more despicable and creatively nasty things…spiraling downward with each incarnation. Between incarnations there is no rest. There is no break from the pursuit of evil. They are fettered to it. He explained that he is so tired. So very tired. He would welcome healing at the Soma banquet which would not only release the soul of the man who sat before me, but release the personages he had been in previous incarnations (before he was Dr Mengela) and those he had become in subsequent incarnations. He accepted my invitation. He was very much of a gentleman and my heart felt compassion for him. My heart also felt compassion for the world and what a better place it was going to be without the repetitious mischief this entity had caused. It occurred to me that this type to healing could thwart the prophecies regarding the return of the Anti-Christ.

Others came.

I recognized that they seemed to fall into one of two categories. The first group was as Dr. Mengela – evil doers who were tired, devoid of hope, never resting, reincarnating over and over getting worse and worse. Their reincarnations required that they develop their "craft".

The second group consisted of those who were naïve, ignorant and completely empty, and their void desperately needed to be filled. This type of spirit is easy prey for the dark energies. These spirits I also invited to come to the Soma banquet to fill their void – their hungry places – with Soma.

4.) Finally I was to invite spirits I have a negative personal relationship with. People alive or dead who hate me, or I hate them. People, alive or dead, whom I have not forgiven or who have not forgiven me.

Again, these spirits fell into two categories.

The first were people I had loved at one time and the love had turned to disappointment and hatred through betrayal in one way or another. Sometimes the betrayal was not even known to the betrayer. They were all invited to the Soma Banquet where we would make amends and remember what it was like to love one another. The memory of the loving times would then remain in our consciousness rather than the acrid bad feelings.

The second group of spirits were ones who annoy me and waste my time. People I don't like to give time to. The Soma Feast was a good place to become more compassionate and realize that it is really only their style that annoys me rather than their actual existence.

The guests were all gathered. The birds had completed their reed basket around the world. All was silent. The Ark of the Covenant hovered at the top of the world above the Soma crater.

First the guests came to drink the healing Soma.

Next the Protectors and Witnesses who had been stationed at all the sacred sites were given a command and in an instant they released the gravity of Earth. Everything fell into the reed basket. The dark cloud of pollution that blankets Indonesia fell into the bottom of the basket and its weight caused the bottom of the reed basket to break open. Powerful

Garudas and bird-deities flew to create a patch in the basket. Elephants came forward to help hold up the bottom of the basket. Meanwhile all the negativity and evil of the world – physical, emotional, historical and political all seeped out of the reed basket and became harmless dust in the atmosphere.

From the four corners of the Ark came four laser beams that cut gorges in the sides of the crater and the Soma lake began to flow into the basket that surrounded earth, soothing, healing and enveloping every country, city, continent and ocean. The Protectors then returned the gravity to earth and after that was done, the reeds that formed the basket around Earth fell away in glorious stripes of white light and stars.

And this non-ordinary reality experience was the culmination of my introduction to the Meditation Buddhas, their Taras and Swayambhu.

But April 3$^{rd}$ was a lost day for me. The creeping discomfort from the day before erupted in a full-fledged gastrointestinal nightmare. It was clear that I was not going to be able to travel far from the "tall toilet" in my room. I was disappointed.

I had been thinking long and hard about the Thangka I had decided to buy and I tried to describe it to Art in an email. It was then that I realized that I could not remember what it looked like and, that being the case, it had not touched my heart. It had not spoken to me! I came down to breakfast for toast and tea and indicated to Larry that the Thangka at Gauri's did not seem to be something I should buy. He understood and said he would relay the message to Gauri. I then fled back to my room just in the nick of time.

There was a heavy fleece blanket on each of the beds in my room. I curled up under both of them and fell into a feverish sleep – the kind that generates bizarre dreams and disorientation. My sickness was unnerving. I was in a strange country on the other side of the world and I knew I had to get better and get re-hydrated post hast or I ran the risk of ending up in a Nepali hospital. I had charcoal tablets and Chinese herbs from my acupuncturist; Nux Vomica from Denise's homeopathic arsenal, a package of Imodium Sarah had given me, and, as a last ditch effort, Cipro (a prescription general-use antibiotic).

For lunch I ordered chicken noodle soup from room service. By mid-afternoon I began to feel better. Sarah and Mujiba called when they returned from Swayambhu and asked if I wanted to go with them to the textile district to order saris and kurtas and I decided to chance it.

I had come to Nepal with every intention of buying a sari while I was here. But I was beginning to have my doubts about how practical it would be for me. I would first have to buy the sari, then a matching petticoat with a tight drawstring waist. I would also need a matching, tight-fitting blouse that ends just below the bust. With these sari essentials you begin by tucking, wrapping and pleating the fabric around the waist, then bringing the fabric under your arm and over the opposite shoulder. The end portion falls to the level of your knees. Safety pins can be used to secure everything, but the entire get-up looked very risky to me. In one short sari lesson I developed a whole new respect for women who wear the elegant garb.

The shop Aama and Ram directed us to consisted of two walls of shelves on which were folded sets of yard goods ready for the tailor. They were arranged by fabric and hence by price. A kurta, rather than a sari, was a much better option for me. A kurta consists of a dress, punjab pants and a matching shawl. Mujiba selected fabric for two kurtas, Sarah found one and they both helped me find the fabric I bought. The one that really caught my eye was turquoise with white flowers, but Sarah pronounced the fabric to be polyester and unacceptable. We then looked in the cotton section and found a lovely rose stripe with gilt threads running through it.

*Bargaining In the Sari/Kurta Shop*
(Taken by Mujiba Cabugos)
*Mujiba getting measured for her kurta*
(Taken by Sue Melanson)

The discarded fabric was flung into a brightly colored pile as we examined the possibilities. We also decided to have a kurta made for Aama as a gift from Sarah, Mujiba and me. After we had selected the fabric the young boy in the shop ran to get the tailor down the street.

Meanwhile, I needed a bathroom and Ram asked the older youth in the shop to take me to it. We stepped out of the shop, entered a long dark hallway between two shops and stepped over a huge pile of rebar. He opened a padlocked door and switched on a bare light bulb. Before me in the floor was a dreaded squat toilet.

When I returned to the shop all measuring was complete and we were selecting necklines and sleeve lengths. The tailor spoke excellent English so we felt confident we would end up with exceptional garments three days hence. But the best surprise came next. The cost of each three-piece fabric set was 800 rupees ($12 US) and the tailor's fee was 250 rupees ($4 US). Such a deal!

But Erica had found an even better deal. She purchased a fleece jacket that had to be the ultimate knock-off. On one side it said "Polartec" and it reversed to the other side that said "Northface".

# CHAPTER 10
## April 4, 2006 TUESDAY
## THE EGG SHAMAN, BHAKTAPUR & PASHMINA SHAWLS

I read a blog post, author unknown, that summed up the way I felt about Tuesday in Nepal:

*"Anesthesia, antiseptics and antibiotics are undoubtedly three of the most important discoveries in the history of medical science, but surely the development of Imodium and similar gut-paralyzing drugs must rank closely behind them. I find it unbelievable that the team behind their development did not receive a Nobel Prize. Two of those beautiful little pills got me through the next day."*

For the reader's future reference Imodium's generic name is Loperamide Hydrochloride and you will want a supply if you go to Nepal.

Today is the birthday of the elephant-headed deity Ganesh. We stopped at the Ganesh shrine, as usual, to receive tika and ask for blessings as we began our day. The keeper of the Ganesh shrine bestowed upon each of us a fresh flower mala to mark the occasion.

*Susan, Sarah, Dr. Larry, Sue and Jeff outside the Ganesh Shrine*
*(Taken by Mujiba Cabugos)*

We began the day at Aama's healing room. As she had instructed, I brought a small plastic bottle for mustard oil. Aama toned mantras over the oil and stirred it with her iron knife. Carefully she poured it into my little bottle and instructed me (through Ram's interpreting) to rub it on my knees every night, stroking down my leg, away from my heart. I am to continue this treatment until the oil is gone. The oil has a kitchen smell to it...not objectionable, but strong

Suju's bus took us to a rural location called Duwakot where the Egg Shaman lives. The egg shaman's real name is Hari Bahadur Khadka and he dispenses healings, divinations and shamanic advice. Before we could see him we had to purchase a small bag of rice and three eggs at a little shop across from his house. They were carefully nestled in a plastic bag.

*Sue's Eggs and Rice*
*(Taken by Mujiba Cabugos)*

After we had our eggs we filed into the Egg Shaman's living room where we sat to wait. The house was new and sunny and quite elegant.

The Egg Shaman business must be very good! A few of us had to use the facilities while we were there and despite the elegant modern house, we were directed to an unlighted outhouse with a squat toilet. I didn't actually see what it looked like until I looked at my digital camera pictures.

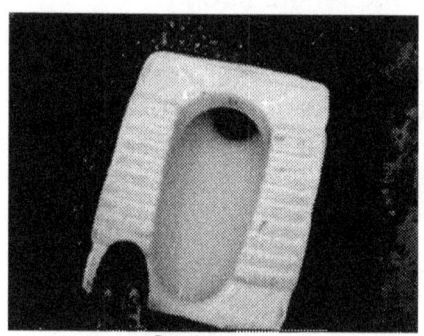
*Squat toilet*
(Taken by Sue Melanson)

Each of us went to see the Egg Shaman individually. Ram was interpreting and stood behind a screen because the Egg Shaman insisted that the interview be between him and the patient privately. I explained that my knees were bothering me. The Egg Shaman stood behind me and cracked an egg. I heard it crack and expected yolk to run down my face – and I had a flashback to Halloween in eighth grade when Dicky Thornquist DID crack an egg on my head. But no yolk came. He then reached behind my knee and appeared to be pulling yards and yards of green twine right out of my knee. He gave me the twine, which was indeed more than would ever have fit inside a chicken egg, and told me to throw it in the river. I thanked him, gave him an offering in rupees and went outside to the others who were also blinking with perplexed expressions. We boarded the bus carrying whatever extraction material he had handed us and drove to a high bridge over a river. With great vigor we hurled our objects into the river. I thought briefly about environmental responsibility, but restrained my conscience in order to fully experience the moment.

We then drove on to Bhaktapur.

Bhaktapur is the former capital of the Kathmandu Valley about 45-minutes east of Kathmandu. The ancient city originated from a string of rural villages along the old trade route from India to Tibet that grew into a flourishing city.

The bus parked in a public parking lot. The brave and the desperate had a chance to face the dreaded squat toilet in a dimly lit shed marked "Tourist Toilet" attended by two Nepali women who held their hands out for a rupee donation.

While we were standing in the parking lot it appeared that the local vendors were acting either under a law or custom that none of them enter the parking lot, but once we passed through the gate we were besieged by entrepreneurs. Some offered to become our guides. Others were selling necklaces, flutes and sarangis, among other things. Sarangis are musical instruments designed to be bowed that look something like crude violins, with a squat, truncated body, a sounding board of goatskin and three main playing strings of heavy gut.

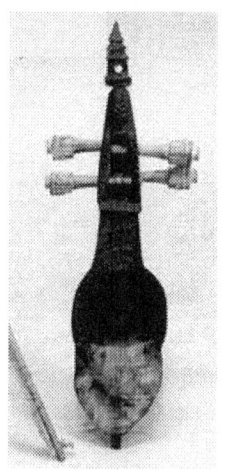

*Sarangi*
*(Taken by Sue Melanson)*

We pushed our way through the crowd to a money booth where we paid a 750-rupee fee (about $11 US) to enter the city. The Bhaktapur Municipality has embarked on an ambitious restoration and preservation project that is financially supported by these fees and they have been successful in reclaiming many of the temples, shrines and palaces that were damaged in the 1934 earthquake. The street vendors eased up as we headed up the hill towards the entrance to Bhaktapur. The long stone steps wound past scattered shops and a shrine or two. I had an "Oh, Yuk!" moment as I stepped hastily over a puddle of fresh blood by one of the shrines. A chicken sacrifice to the deity had apparently been recently made.

*The water truck arrives at Bhaktapur*
(Taken by Mujiba Cabugos)

At the top of the hill a crowd was pressing forward to receive water from a tanker truck. Women and girls rushed forward carrying water containers. This was a daily ritual for them so it did not have the air of impatience one would expect in the US. We passed the water bearers and entered Durbar Square. Here we encountered a different crowd. Students in school uniforms had gathered for examinations. They were enjoying a lunch break and discussing the rigors of the tests amongst themselves.

We passed the National Art Gallery housed in an ancient structure called The 55-Window Palace. This had been the royal palace prior to 1769 AD. The Gallery was closed for renovation as a part of the revival program. In conjunction with this program all vehicles are banned from Durbar Square, which gave the area a museum atmosphere.

There are two bells, side by side, in Durbar Square. The smaller one is called the "Barking Dog Bell" because its pitch causes all dogs around it to whine when it is rung.

What I had not found to be peaceful in Pashupatinath, I found here. The sun was high and the air was clear and, even though there was a bustle of activity, it felt peaceful. I must clarify that "peaceful" does not mean there was not a military presence. That was just a fact of life wherever we went. There was an undercurrent of energy and timelessness that bespeaks the antiquity of the place. I half expected Indiana Jones to come barreling around the corner in his search for Marion Ravenwood who had been reported running a gin mill in Nepal. ("Raiders of the Last Ark").

We moved on toward Taumadhi Square.

*Nyatapola Temple in Bhaktapur*
*(Taken by Sue Melanson)*

Dominating Taumadhi Square is the Nyatapola Temple, a five-tiered pagoda dedicated to the Hindu goddess Siddhi Lakshmi. She is the wrathful manifestation of the Goddess Durga. The temple rests on a base of five levels with four Ganesh shrines in each of the corners. Nyatapola means "five-story temple" in the Newari language. Legend tells of the days when the angry god Bhairab was causing havoc in society. Bhairab's temple stood in Taumadhi Square. To counteract his destructive behavior the king decided to build a more powerful temple right in front of the Bhairab Temple. To make the brick and wood temple strong, King Bhupatendra Malla ordered guardians be placed in pairs on each level of the base leading up to the new temple. On the first level a pair of likenesses of

Bhaktapur's strongest man, Jaya mal Pata, a famous wrestler. Next, two elephants followed by two lions, two griffins and finally "Singhini" and "Baghini", the tiger and lion goddesses. After subduing Bhairab, peace prevailed in the city. The temple is the tallest temple in Kathmandu Valley. It was so well designed that it withstood the powerful 8.3 earthquake in 1934. The image of Siddhi Lakshmi is locked within the temple and only the priests are allowed to enter to worship her.

A huge chariot was being constructed in the middle of Taumadhi Square for the White Macchendranath Festival procession just a few days away. Workmen hoisted panels to the top levels while children played on the lower ones. It reminded me of the colossal Trojan horse.

*Chariot in Bhaktapur*
*(Taken by Mujiba Cabugos)*

We decided to go shopping in several groups and meet back at the chariot at the specified time. Each of the groups took an interpreter /barterer with them. Bhaktapur is an artisan capital with many high quality items we would not find elsewhere. We found shops that specialized in bells, cymbals, doorbells, wind chimes and gongs. Shops that sold stone carvings. There were images of deities available in a variety of forms from Thangkas, to silver statues, to mass-produced resin and bronze "tourist" deities. There were wood carving shops that sold intricately crafted wood printing blocks, figurines and wall hangings called "peacock windows".

*Peacock window in a shop in Bhaktapur*
(Taken by Sue Melanson)

I joined Ram's group as we headed for the pashmina store. Pashmina is remarkably soft wool that is made from the underbelly wool of Kashmir goats and blended with silk. It is commonly made into shawls and scarves. I was on a Pashmina Mission! My daughter was getting married in September and I had promised to bring back shawls for each of her bridesmaids in colors matching their gowns. I had tucked wee fabric samples of the gowns in my wallet. Five of us descended on the pashmina store just east of Taumadhi Square. Sarah was our textile expert and she showed us what to look for. I was looking for six matching shawls -- plain, un-beaded, and unembellished shawls that the girls could use for the rest of their lives. (How optimistic!). I could match either the chocolate brown satin swatch, or the champagne satin swatch. I found a rich brown shawl that radiated "espresso", but there was only one. That would be for our maid of honor. With Sarah's help we found five cream colored shawls that not only matched the swatch, but matched each other. Sarah had also showed us a type of shawl called "water pashmina", which is an ultra light, two-toned variation. I picked out a jewel-toned shawl that was deep rose on one side and orchid on the other for the bride. Not for the wedding, but because she is my dearest, darling daughter. Ram bartered for me and I left the shop triumphant. MISSION ACCOMPLISHED!

Erica had not been looking or feeling well. While we were in the pashmina shop she sat quietly on a chair the shopkeeper brought for her. By the time we joined the others, poor Erica was really unstable. Larry had Cipro and he gave one to Erica. Suju then escorted her back to the bus where she could lay down across the back seat.

The rest of us headed slowly back towards the bus, stopping to take pictures and investigate shops. The side streets were shaded and cool. I caught sight of a serene Nepali woman resting on her elbows in a second story window. She was wearing a red shawl and had an ethereal look on her face. I flipped my camera open and I was just about to capture the artistic shot of the day, when she leaned forward and spit.

Larry found a butter-soft leather jacket that he fell in love with. The problem was that he was not in the market for a casual jacket. He needed a dress jacket. The shop owner was insistent that that was not a problem. He could take Larry's measurements and within a couple of days he would have the jacket re-made to Larry's specifications. You can't say the Nepali vendors aren't customer friendly!

Mujiba bought some elegant handmade paper. Denise and Susan found a drum shop where they were introduced to ocean drums. They are shallow and have stones inside that produce a water sound when held flat and shaken side to side, similar to the action you would make if sifting sand through a strainer. They also looked at a damaru, which is a small two-headed drum that is twisted to swing stones that are attached by strings.

Everyone returned from Bhaktapur with goodies.

Erica, however, was down for the count and when we got closer to the hotel, Larry put her in a taxi with Ram and sent her ahead to the hotel.

# CHAPTER 11
## April 5, 2006 WEDNESDAY
## SHOPPING IN BOUDDHANATH, LUNCH WITH THE CHINEA LAMA AND CARPETS

Denise discovered Tibetan French Toast at breakfast. It is a plate-size, deep-fried raised-donut thing. There are slits in it so it cooks in the middle but the slits give it an oriental symbol look and it is served with honey and cherry (always cherry) jelly. I stuck to porridge and toast, but had a taste of Denise's delicacy.

Suju was waiting for us with the bus. The Ganesh priest was waiting for us with tika and blessings. And Aama was waiting for us with big news. We have established a veritable pattern of behavior!

On the way to Aama's the bus passed by the university and the king's palace and it seemed like there were many more uniformed personnel in evidence. The tension was greater, too. No longer were the soldiers leaning against trees or sitting on walls. They were on their feet, alert and at the ready.

In Aama's neighborhood the women were still pounding laundry under the water spigot, the thin water buffs were still thin, and the curious children with big dark eyes and mischievous smiles were still calling "Hello, Hello!" And Aama's healing room was crowded as usual.

Aama's clients came and went.

The Calcutta lady with the wanderlust brother-in-law came for yet another bottle of anti-love-potion whiskey. She reported positive change in her sister's situation. The first night the husband drank the anti-love-potion he left his home to go to "The Other Woman". The next day he lingered at home for a while before leaving. Then last night he slept at home, in his own bed, with his own wife. And now "The Other Woman" was calling his house wanting to know where he was. Aama's treatment was working!

After everyone had been seen, including those in our group, the BIG news was announced.

Aama and Pramod have been issued 5-year US visas. Being a member of The International Council of Thirteen Indigenous Grandmothers has been a big help getting this for

Aama. And Pramod will be her interpreter. Several years ago Larry's people had worked hard to get Pramod to the United States. Pramod had been accepted to a college in the US and everything was in place, except that vital little piece of paper...a visa. Aama and Pramod were wasting no time in taking advantage of their opportunity to move around, either. They already had flight reservations to California April 23. The opportunities and implications for Pramod were huge. He wants to move to the US with his wife and baby and all indications appear to be leading him in that direction.

In honor of the Big News, Larry made reservations at a Thai Restaurant for dinner to celebrate. From Aama's we walked to the Bouddhanath Stupa. Most of us had mastered the learning curve of recognizing the rupee/US dollar ratio with the help of a conversion chart Susan created. We had become comfortable with the goods that were available and everyone in the group were about to become Shopping Divas. The shops and vendors that encircled the Stupa were our playground.

I teamed up with Jeff who was in search of a gurkha knife for his 24-year-old son. A gurkha or khukuri, is a medium-length curved knife. The scabbard is often decorated with silver and has two pockets to hold two tiny knives tucked behind. One is used to cut small things and the other is a sharpener. The original Gurkhas were the elite fighting force of India's army. The elite of the Nepali army are also called Gurkhas. It is said that when gurkha knives were used in battle the owner would intentionally cut himself with the knife because they did not want the knife to go into battle without having drawn blood.

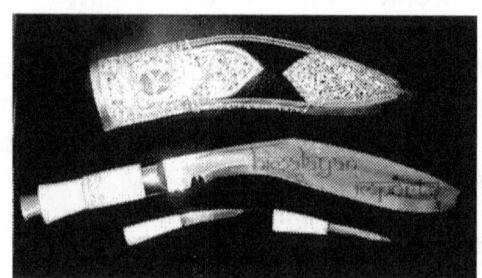

*Gurkha Knife*
*(Taken by Sue Melanson)*

I was looking for family gifts and a Ganesh statue for my own altar. We roamed from shop to shop. In one establishment I discovered a tiny image of Ganesh just two inches high cast in green resin to look like jade. The detail was good and the price was right.

*Faux jade Ganesh*
(Taken by Sue Melanson)

As we walked we were inadvertently circumambulating the stupa. I observed dozens of people with wooden trowels crouched on the first level of the stupa busily refinishing the stucco surface in preparation for Buddha's birthday celebration.

*New stucco for the Bouddhanath Stupa*
(Taken by Mujiba Cabugos)

Prayer flags were being added to the hundreds already fluttering in the breeze and people could write prayers, names or messages on the new ones for a donation.

Sometimes in my life I have stood before an opportunity and for one reason or another I haven't taken it. In our browsing Jeff and I discovered a wonderful woman selling her wares on tables in a side alley. She spoke perfect English. I was looking for a Durga statue and she didn't have any, but almost as if she was reading my mind she directed me to other merchandise she felt I might like that included a small bronze singing bowl and two quartz crystal pillars about 6" high with layers of red clay in the base. She said she would try to bring a Durga statue the next day. I told her I hoped to come back the next day. She bowed gently and said, "I am a very poor woman and you have money that will help me." It wasn't begging. It wasn't pressure sales. It was a simple statement of fact and she made her point and I understood. I almost bought the singing bowl and the crystals there and then, but I didn't, and I have regretted it ever since. I never got back to the Bouddhanath Stupa again and I never found my vendor lady again.

In a shop by the gate I ducked into one final shop and found necklaces made of strings of tiny glass beads with carved bone spacers. The necklaces lay like a collar around my neck. I bought one made of black beads with elephants carved on the spacers for myself, and another made of deep indigo blue beads for my sister, Joan.

We gathered at the appointed time because we didn't want to be late for lunch with the Chinea Lama and his family.

The Chinea Lama is the head of the Tibetan Buddhist community at Bouddhanath and his given name is Ganesh. He is both a religious and a political figure and a very old and dear friend of Larry's. He is also Jigme's father.

*The Chinea Lama*
(Taken by Mujiba Cabugos)

Jigme and his mother greeted us and we passed through a tidy garden lorded over by a fluffy little white dog. We were ushered into a cool, comfortable living room to await the arrival of the Chinea Lama. Larry's friendship with this family has, over the years, opened many doors for him within Nepal.

The Chinea Lama and his wife (one of his wives) had recently been to New York and had many observations about his trip. Our visit was very jovial and relaxed. Female members of the Chinea Lama's family served lunch and a strikingly pretty girl in pink was very attentive to Larry. I could not tell whether she was flirting with him or worshiping him...perhaps both.

Besides being a part of Larry's staff, Jigme runs the Whyzer Tibetan Carpet factory. He is extremely proud of the quality of the carpets he produces and the creative energy that goes into each one. After lunch we had a chance to view some of his creations. A couple of boys brought each rolled carpet in and laid it out for our inspection. The colors, the intricate designs, the density (100 knots hand tied) and the subtle carving around the patterns were breathtaking. Jigme had a lot to be proud of. Most of the carpets were about 4' x 6', but Jigme had been telling us about the little rabbit fur rugs he had recently made. There were two, about the size of the seat of a large chair and soft as a little bunny. Mujiba bought them both for $100 US each. I was not in the market for a carpet for myself, but my cousin's daughter was getting married and I was considering something tastefully neutral for her wedding present. I live in a house of braided country rugs and wall-to-wall carpet so I did not consider that I needed a carpet. Then I saw it – the lavender dragon!

*The Lavender Dragon carpet*
*(Taken by Sue Melanson)*

I drew my knees up to my chin and gazed at it. The recent Thangka fiasco was fresh in my mind and I wanted to make a good decision. My friend Joahnna had told me she believed I would be sitting in front of something during my trip that I could not rationalize financially. She predicted this moment! I also remembered Art's tale of acquiring a Persian carpet on one of his early shipping adventures. The Persian carpet had survived both of his previous marriages and now lay on our library floor…on TOP of the wall-to-wall carpet. I think my voice squeaked as I asked "How much?" It was $410US. My mind whirled "That's ALL?" But in that moment Jeff was also falling in love with the Lavender Dragon. As luck would have it, Jigme had another dragon almost complete in the workshop. He could have it ready before we left. So both Jeff and I made our decisions and TWO Lavender Dragons were spoken for. Larry was pleased. He liked bringing business to Jigme and he had found two carpets, one for himself and one for his newlywed son, Aaron. He had purchased a smaller version of the Lavender Dragon for his daughter, Jemma, years before.

We continued to look over Jigme's wares and I spotted the carpet I would have bought for Jennifer's wedding gift. It was a swirl design made up of neutral earth colors. And it was much bigger than the other carpets. It was 7' x 10'. The prospect of carrying it in my luggage all the way to Maine was daunting. But the price was right and I thought long and hard about it, but in the end, I left it behind.

Before we left, the Chinea Lama blessed each of us with a white silk Tibetan prayer scarf called a katag, woven with the symbols of the eight Buddhist auspicious signs.

Jigme's mother, whom he called "Mummy", offered to show us Jigme's brother's monastery, which was next door. Her "offer to show us" was more of a command and we did not want to disobey Mummy. The Rinpoche, Jigme's brother, was visiting his monastery in Canada at the moment. A Rinopoche is a re-incarnation of a lama. In this case he is Tulku incarnate. Tibetan Buddhism consists of five main sects: Ningma, Sakya, Kagyu, Gelu and Benbo. The Chinea Lama is a member of the Ningma sect. In the early 19th century, the King of Nepal officially declared that the Chinea Lama lineage would function as the officiating religious body at the Bouddhanath Stupa for the local Tamang, Newari and Tibetan community.

After leaving our street shoes outside the monastery doors, we began our tour in the Waiting Room where Mummy explained the rigors of the spiritual exercises they engage in daily. To start, the household sits in lotus position meditating for an hour. The legs are crossed with left foot on right thigh, right foot on left thigh soles facing up. Hands are placed in the lap, palms up with the thumb and forefinger joined. Once in position, one sits tall like a tree with great dignity. The very words "lotus position" made the long muscles of my outer thighs cringe. After they complete their meditation, they proceed to the Shrine Room, which is dominated by several exquisite Buddha images and the Rinpoche's throne. Mummy explained that they do 108 prostrations in front of Buddha. She stood erect, flung her arms back, brought her palms together in prayer, then dropped to her knees, stretched forward into a fully prone position, then hopped up and did it again. Ganesh (The Chinea Lama) is in his 80's. Mummy, his second wife, had to be in her 50's or 60's. I was impressed! But then she broke the spell by suggesting...suggesting with force...that we try it. She wanted each of us to do five...only five. Sarah turned to the door and vocalized what we were all thinking: "I don't THINK so."

In the high-ceilinged, marble hallway Mummy had laid out silk brocade slippers for us to wear for the rest of the tour. I picked a pair that looked like they fit and slid into them. No sooner were my toes happily inside when I looked up and discovered the glowering countenance of Mummy looking up at me. I had taken HER slippers! Opps!! I quickly took them off and instead of looking for another pair I grabbed the moment to slide out the door into the courtyard as Mujiba, who had been taking pictures outside, came sliding in the door. Suju's bus was parked by a giant one-story prayer wheel. Larry, Jigme, Ram and Suju were having a smoke with the Chinea Lama, so I climbed on board and slid low in my seat in case Mummy was watching out of the second floor windows. When everyone returned to the bus we had to laugh since Mummy got Mujiba to do the prostrations. I guess someone had to do them for all of us!

We were all tired. The day had been hotter than others and dustier, but I refused to let my body crash early. I felt it was important to celebrate Aama and Pramod's visa status. Denise had some wonderful little coffee flavored candies that were loaded with caffeine and perfect for a situation like this.

The Yin Yang Thai Restaurant is entered through a pretty courtyard with a bakery to the left. We climbed stone steps to the upper level where a low table surrounded by floor pillows was set for us. We were in a bow window and, even though my aching legs would not fold under me, I was propped against the wall and the open windows wafted cool evening air into the room. I ordered Phad Thai, a dish of stir-fried rice noodles with eggs, fish sauce, tamarind juice, red chili pepper, bean sprouts, shrimp and chicken. It is garnished with crushed peanuts, cilantro and a wedge of lime. I ordered it because I had had it before and knew, in general, what to expect when the order came. It was the best I have ever had. It was mildly spicy but not overwhelming. Denise and I shared a beer. Pramod sat next to me and was being carefully observed by two tables of young ladies. One group of four was from the US and the other pair from the Netherlands. Pramod, who is an expert at picking out eye-candy, had himself become eye-candy.

Each evening, before bed, I try to send an email from the computer room to all my fans summing up my day. I can wrestle with Computer One with the letters and numerals worn off the keys or Computer Two with the space bar that sticks. I have to log in to our server's website half a world away in Maine. I can see the local time at the bottom of my screen and the Maine time in the corner of the Points South website - over 10 hours difference. After checking any incoming messages, summing up my day to a handful of my interested fans, I try to let Art and Krissie know how much I miss them. Some days I am more homesick than others. Today was more. I drifted off to sleep with a song echoing in my head:

*Let me go home*
*I'm just too far from where you are*
*I want to come home*
*And I feel just like I'm living someone else's life*
*It's like I just stepped outside*
*When everything was going right*
*And I know just why you could not*
*Come along with me*
*That this is not your dream*
*But you always believed in me*

Michael Buble

# CHAPTER 12
## April 6, 2006 THURSDAY
## THE BANDHA, CURFEW AND ERICA'S HOSPITALITY

Today is the Festival of the White Macchendranath, the Buddhist deity of rain. Traditionally, the Seto (white) Macchendranath god is cleaned, painted and perfumed. A special chariot is prepared and the living goddess Kumari visits him. It is believed that if the god is pleased with the worship, the people in the valley will have a prosperous year.

But we didn't see any of it.

Today is also the first day of the nationwide four-day bandha (general strike) which was called by the Seven Party Alliance representing the elected parties of the now dissolved parliament. The object of the strike is to force the king into restoring a multi-party democratic system. There were skirmishes between police and groups of demonstrators who threw rocks and played "catch-me-if-you-can" near the university and the palace.

*This is a picture of the TV screen in my room.*
*I was certainly not in the streets this close to the action.*
*(Taken by Sue Melanson)*

Stores were closed and there were no vehicles on the streets. I assume "vehicles" also applied to the huge chariot on which the White Macchendranath processes. We have heard that there will be a mass demonstration on Saturday.

Larry has seen these strikes before and they don't last long and have never affected tourists. The Thamel district is pretty much sacrosanct and Westerners are left alone. Hotel vehicles identify themselves with TOURISTS ONLY signs and can move about.

But this bandha is different.

We came down for breakfast and a hand written sign was taped to the front desk in the lobby that read: Curfew 9 AM until 4 PM. It was enforceable by the police and the army, so Larry advised us to stay in the hotel during curfew hours. We are also hampered because Larry's staff was unable to get to us.

Sometime during the hours of our confinement I wandered down to the cyber room to see if anyone from the other side of the world had sent me a message. As I passed through the lobby a police van pulled into the courtyard and a bevy of Westerners climbed out and made their way into the lobby talking loudly amongst themselves and causing quite a commotion. It appeared that the police had picked up the group in Durbar Square where a sizeable crowd of demonstrators was gathering.

We met with Larry on the roof in the early afternoon and we shared tidbits of news we had heard. I told him about the police vanload of Westerners. He asked how many there were and I reported 20 or so. I hadn't actually taken a head count. He wanted to know why they had been brought in. I didn't know, but from their raucous mood I had assumed they were not brought in of their own accord.

Later in the day Erica, fully recovered from her ailment, invited all of us to her room for a party. Erica's room had a stocked refrigerator and she willingly allowed us to select whatever we wanted to drink. Most of her offerings were soda (or "pop" if you come from certain parts of the US). The soda comes in timeworn 8-oz glass bottles that had obviously been recycled over and over again and had that haze you see on beach glass.

Erica had not been well enough to join us the day before in Bouddhanath. She had spiked a fever, but towards mid-afternoon felt well enough to venture forth on her own. She tried to locate a shop called "P.T. Lama's" only to discover that Lama is the Nepali equivalent to Smith or Jones. She did, however, find a small shop that sold crystal phurbas. A phurba is a ritual dagger with a three-sided blade that is useful in various types of shamanic rituals. The salesman told her he had a box for the phurba in his storeroom and invited Erica to come pick one out. It was either a grand sense of adventure, a little leftover fever, or the fact that Erica had come of age in the 60's and was very trusting. In any case, she followed the shopkeeper up a long spiral ladder, past some nasty barking Tibetan dogs, to his storeroom and picked out the box she wanted.

As Erica told her story Susan and Mujiba doubled over laughing. They decided that "Come up and see my phurba!" is the Nepali version of "Come up and see my etchings!"

We sat in a circle enjoying our libation and Erica showed us the exquisite crystal phurba. We decided to use the phurba as a talking stick and passed it one to the other as we told stories of things that have happened to us.

I chose to share one of my earliest experiences in non-ordinary reality. I shared the story about my trip around the Gaspe Peninsula in Canada over ten years ago before I learned how to walk in both ordinary and non-ordinary reality. My husband and I were traveling the winding road that hugs the rocky cliffs overhanging the Gulf of Saint Lawrence. The road is narrow and rises to the top of the bluffs, then descends to the edge of the sea. We rounded a bend and could see a cluster of cars ahead of us near the top of a cliff. There had been an accident and we proceeded slowly as a self-appointed traffic control person waved us by. A motorcycle had skidded off the pavement and under the guardrail. Two passers-by were holding the injured biker by the arms as his bike slid out from under him and over the edge of the cliff. We inched past the scene, trying not to be rubber-neckers. As we came close to the biker his eyes met mine for an instant and we were connected. Not knowing what was happening, I drew my legs up in a semi lotus position, palms up, and closed my eyes and began to rock. Art noticed that something was going on but he didn't know what. We cleared the traffic jam and proceeded down the road. Art commented that an ambulance should be coming our way soon. I responded that the ambulance had already come up from the other direction and the biker, terrified, was en route to the hospital. I realized in that instant that I was connected to the biker in non-ordinary reality and I could be the biker's intermediary. My guides (although I did not know I had guides at the time) wanted to use my Third Eye to tune into the Universe, but I resisted. There was no time to educate me, so my guides simply opened my crown chakra and the information flowed freely. The biker feared that his back was broken and that the men who had rescued him might have injured him further. My awareness increased and I flashed back the information he needed. Both men were off-duty EMT's and had handled him properly. I likewise pulled information from the ether that his back was, indeed, not broken and that his injury, although serious, was not life threatening. The biker was also worried about his family. Would the accident be on the news? He had been, apparently, somewhere he was not supposed to be and feared they would not know it was him…or maybe they would. I don't know which prospect concerned him more. I was able to "tell" him that his daughter had been contacted and she was on her way to the hospital to meet the ambulance. They had taken his contact information from his wallet. He wanted to know if they had taken his money, too, and I answered, "No, they had not. They are professionals." My connection continued. I could feel pain in my own back. Art had read extensively and was aware of this kind of phenomena, although the whole experience was uncharted territory for us. In conversation Art realized that I was becoming more and more disoriented in my own reality and heavily connected to the biker's precarious position. Art pulled the car into a rest area and said very softly and very gently, "You have to break this connection. You have done what you can." In listening to Art's words, I realized that he was right. I had done all I could. And as easily as that, by simply willing it, the connection was broken.

    I returned to the cyber room later in the evening and June poked her head in to inform me, in no uncertain terms, that my report about the police van was wrong. Dead wrong! The group was fourteen not twenty and they had requested transport out of the danger zone. She had gotten the facts and wanted to set me straight. What an abrasive personality!

Tomorrow we are hoping to see Durbar Square and do some shopping, but, as we have seen, every day dawns here with a degree of unpredictability.

# CHAPTER 13
## April 7, 2006 FRIDAY
## DURBAR SQUARE AND THE YIN YANG RESTAURANT

The strike continued into its second day. Employees of the banks have left work chanting slogans in favor of democracy, and today doctors and nurses, still in uniform, paramedics and medical students gathered expressing solidarity with the anti-monarchy movement. A local news commentator pointed out that doctors are a powerful group to reckon with and are usually the last professional group to show up [at demonstrations]. Meanwhile, Maoists rebels had taken advantage of the unrest and launched simultaneous attacks on all security installations in the towns of Butwal and Toulihawa. In Kathmandu it is suspected that Maoists are behind the vandalism, violence and arson that has occurred in an attempt to provoke security forces to open fire on the demonstrators causing a mass revolt in the streets.

We can sometimes hear the sounds of the crowds from Larry's rooftop location, but they sounded far away. It is anticipated that the demonstrations are taking place near the king's palace and the university. The Thamel district, where our hotel is located, is regarded as a tourist district and we don't expect the demonstrations to come into Thamel.

Larry decided we can safely venture forth to see the sights in Durbar Square, which is the heart of Kathmandu and full of old palaces, temples and shrines, and within reasonable walking distance of the hotel.

Before we got to Durbar Square we passed a Ganesh temple and decided to stop to ensure that our day go forward smoothly. On many temples and shrines you will see mounted mirrors. The idea is to scare off evil spirits and sorcerers by showing them their own countenances. While we waited our turn to enter, Gauri and Pramod were observed preening in the evil spirit mirrors. Pramod was checking his teeth and Gauri was slicking down his thick eyebrows.

*Military presence in Durbar Square*
*(Taken by Mujiba Cabugos)*

The military presence on the way to Durbar Square was significant and we saw new military uniforms with white sashes just like we wore in the Warren School crossing guard corps. The king and queen are not in Kathmandu today. They are in Birgunj near the border of India at the World Hindu Conference.

When we arrived in Durbar Square we stopped at a ticket booth to pay the contribution requested of 200 rupees ($3 US) for which we received a souvenir ticket and a comprehensive pamphlet of the area.

Our first stop was the open-air pavilion Kasthamandap Temple, built with the wood from a single sal tree. Kasthamandap means, literally, "made of wood". It was cool and dark under the two-story roof. The central image is the Indian guru, Gorakhnath, the originator of yoga and meditation, and the statue is covered in auspicious vermilion ochre. The name Gorakhnath means a person who has mastered his senses and has complete control over the five negative characteristics in human nature: sexuality, temper, ego, greed and worldly attachment. He is the patron saint of the monarchy. His footprints are also cast in stone – or maybe it was concrete. A beggar on crutches had taken up sentinel duty within the railing that surrounded the statue.

*Goraknath Image at the Kasthamandap Temple*
(Taken by Mujiba Cabugos)

We were then drawn to a huge kneeling Garuda statue outside the temple dedicated to Vishnu. Garuda (Eagle Man) is Vishnu's "vehicle" and is usually portrayed as a bird-like creature that eats serpents and other things that are in his way.

*Garuda Statue in Durbar Square*
(Taken by Sue Melanson)

Legend tells how Garuda's mother was trapped and held by serpents of the lower world. They demanded soma, the elixir of immortality, as ransom. Garuda was told to fly to the moon where the soma was kept and bring some back. This was the key to his mother's release. So Garuda flew to the moon and begged Chandra, the keeper of the soma storehouse, for the soma and he received it, carrying it in his beak and flew back. When he returned Vishnu asked how much of the soma he had taken for himself. Garuda said he never thought of it because this soma was for his mother's release. Vishnu was so impressed with Garuda's honesty and lack of ego that he made him his vehicle ever after.

This particular Garuda image had a man's face and body and huge wings. It was monumental in size and I found myself mesmerized as I stood in its shadow. If I were to select my favorite Nepali deity image, this would probably be the one.

According to my handy guide pamphlet, behind the Vishnu Temple (officially called the Trailokya Mohan Narayan Temple) is the Kumari's Palace.

The story goes that an ancient king of Nepal was passing time playing a game of dice with Taleju, an exquisitely beautiful goddess who gave advice and power to the monarch. As they played he began to secretly lust after her. This was not a good thing because Taleju, being a goddess, could read his mind. She abruptly ended the game and told the king that he would never be able to speak with her again unless she was in the form and body of a very young virgin. This manifestation of the goddess Taleju is the Kumari. The Kumari is a pre-pubescent girl who is chosen as the "Living Goddess", the living version of Taleju. Nine-year-old Preeti Shakya has been worshipped as the Kumari since she was four. The girl selected to be the Kumari must belong to the Buddhist Shakya clan, a sparse community of goldsmiths. Her family background must be impeccable, and the candidate must be calm, poised and fearless. She must possess thirty-two characteristics of physical perfection which include the following: Her skin must be blemish-free; Her hair and eyes, very black; Her body has to be sturdy as a Banyan tree; Her thighs like those of a deer; Her neck like a conch-shell; Her tongue, small and moist; She must have no bad body odors; Her voice must be crystal clear; Her hands and feet dainty; Her sexual organs small and well recessed; and she shall have lost no teeth. Her horoscope must in no way conflict with that of the king. As a little girl she undergoes an emotionally charged initiation during which she must sit in a circle of 108 slain water buffalo and not flinch, cry out, faint or show any sign of hysteria. Once installed, she is guarded by a priestess, and carried around so she does not fall and cut herself. If she bleeds her tenure ends. After she reaches puberty and starts her first menstrual cycle, she returns to regular life. This fall from grace has never been smooth. Parents have little use for a daughter they hardly know with no social or domestic skills, no education, and slim prospects of finding a husband due to the popular belief that the husband of a former Kumari will die young. Recently the government has seen fit to provide the Kumari with reading and writing skills so she will not be totally helpless in society. We hoped to catch a glimpse of the little girl goddess in one of the third floor windows of her palace, but luck was not with us.

We proceeded past various temples and came upon the White Bhairab Temple.

*White Bhairab Temple in Durbar Square*
(Taken by Sue Melanson)

Bhairab represents Shiva in his destructive manifestation. The gilt image is mounted behind a wooden screen that is only raised once in awhile during festivals. At that time the White Bhairab's mouth is filled with beer and devotees drink through long straws. We were lucky. The wooden screen was raised and a priest was perched beside the deity ready to sell the long straws. With a stern fatherly air, Larry recommended we NOT partake.

Across the way is the Jagannath Temple dedicated to Lord Krishna. The roof struts are carved with scenes from the Karma Sutra (i.e. erotic art). Unfortunately the exterior of the

Temple was being renovated and the famous carvings were obscured behind bamboo scaffolding. We could, however, buy postcards just about anywhere in Kathmandu showing the carvings in intimate detail. (Those same postcard dealers sold a postcard of live elephants copulating. Did you ever wonder how they did it?)

We next found ourselves in front of a statue of the kneeling figure of Hanuman, the Hindu monkey god, beside the main door of the Hanuman Dhoka Palace. I thought Erica was going to break into a jig when she saw it, she was so excited – Hanuman is her favorite guy! This is the original royal palace and the traditional heart of the old city. When King Gyanendra ascended to the throne in 2001, his coronation was here.

*Sarah approaches the Black Bhairab*
*(Taken by Sue Melanson)*

We all gathered near the Black Bhairab (Kal Bhairav), which is a massive stone carving of Shiva in his destructive manifestation. The figure was found buried in a farmer's field north of the city. Can you imagine driving your John Deere over something like this? This is where government officials are sworn in and they risk the wrath of Kal Bhairav if they screw up. That, of course, was when there WERE government officials to swear in.

There were military vehicles parked everywhere and Larry advised us to just keep moving along. We eyed the military watchers and they eyed us. We didn't speak. We didn't smile. We just moved along.

As we moved back towards the hotel, Pramod stopped at a spice dealer. The prettier the vendor, the more likely we were to stop.

*Pramod and the spice dealer*
*(Taken by Sue Melanson)*

He was cooking dinner for Larry that evening and he wanted to pick up some mushrooms and spices. After Pramod had purchased what he needed, he pointed out other wares the young lady had to sell. There was a special salt recommended for sore throats. Another spice called Timbur was a very strong, anaesthetizing pod about the size of the head of a clove (the kind you imbed in the Easter ham). Pramod told us it was good for respiratory problems. I tried a single pod and I couldn't feel my lips or tongue for a half hour.

As we walked, Gauri and I had a chance to talk for the first time since I had reneged on the Durga thangka. I tried to explain to Gauri how the thangka had not touched me in my heart. I could not, in fact, remember its details. He seemed to understand, but his polite silence made me feel like pond scum. My change of heart represented a hefty chunk of change for him.

We poked into alleyways and courtyards, called "chowks", and I was able to find a little shop selling pods of "soul flowers". Larry has cited these as being Narling Mendo flowers from the Bignascia tree, but I can't find references to either. The pods are about 18" long and filled with hundreds of luminous soul flowers. I bought two pods and I regret that I will be unable to bring them home. We aren't allowed to take seedpods through customs. I waited until our last day in Nepal and transferred the soul flowers to an envelope marked "Paper Flowers" and discarded the pods, but not before I captured them with my camera.

*Soul Flower Seed Pods*
*(Taken by Sue Melanson)*

There were neighborhood temples and shrines tucked here and there all over Kathmandu. Several of us stumbled upon a small stupa complete with prayer flags and prayer wheels. A keyhole opening in a little shrine caught Mujiba's attention and she put her eye right up to the hole only to find a very large cockroach staring back at her.

Our kurtas are ready! Ram accompanied Sarah, Mujiba and I to the textile district and the tailor's shop. Mujiba had selected a lime green fabric with some interesting texture and embroidery on it. There was an imperfection because light had bleached out a section of the fabric, but the tailor was able to construct her garment to eliminate the flaw. I was impressed! Sarah's needed a minor alteration, which was done while we waited. My kurta is so elegant that I almost hesitate to wear it. I can't wait to see Aama's face when we present her with her brand new kurta…a special gift just from Sarah, Mujiba and I.

That afternoon we had our usual meeting with Larry on the roof and everyone offered their observations and anything else they had learned. I had read an article about a TOURIST ONLY vehicle being attacked. No one was hurt, but the car was damaged. TOURIST ONLY vehicles have been left alone in the past. I began to think about sharing it until I recalled June's vicious correction of my news from the previous day. After everyone had spoken, I hesitated and then prefaced my news tidbit with the fact that the manner in which June accosted me in the cyber room left me feeling like I really did not want to share anything further with the group. June responded by chopping air with her hand as she gritted her teeth: "I just wanted to set Sue straight." Perhaps we are all just a little on edge. The situation here is certainly unnerving. But it also could be that June is just an unpleasant person. She has not shown me any other face than the nasty one thus far.

Erica has taken to telling people to say "Paneer" when taking photographs. Paneer is a kind of soft cheese used in cooking. It seems to get the same facial expression as "Cheese" or "Sex". (Ah ha, I caught you, the Reader, mouthing the words to see if I am right!)

Sarah had forewarned us to bring ginger chews with us to counteract upset stomach. I couldn't find any at home so I picked up a tin of Ginger Altoids. Denise discovered that a single ginger Altoid dissolved in a liter bottle of water is a very tasty beverage.

We were able to move about by dinnertime and we went to the same Yin Yang Thai restaurant we had gone to before. This time Larry took pity on those of us with arthritic knees and asked for a table with chairs. June sat directly across from me and there was icy silence between us. Not even a generic, "Please pass the butter." But her attitude did not dampen the spirits of the rest of the group. Dinner was very jovial and we laughed heartily and drank a lot of beer. Denise ordered a Hot Toddy after dinner and we all envied her choice, but realistically knew we had to walk back to the hotel.

# CHAPTER 14
## April 8, 2006 SATURDAY
## WHAT WE ARE MISSING & TAGLIATELLI VERDE

There is a curfew in Kathmandu again from 7 AM until 8 PM, and today is supposed to be the beginning of the big demonstration. Our original plan was to go to Pokhara by bus for three nights, but with all the unrest Larry has decided to take us by plane. The bus ride would have taken us through some interesting landscapes similar to those in the movie "Romancing The Stone" (except that was South America). There is a possibility of landslides and blocked roads, but there is also the chance of being stopped by Maoist rebels. The Maoists have been extorting money from tourists in various places and trekkers are especially at risk. We had hoped to take a cable car to the mountaintop shrine of Manakamina on the way to Pokhara, but missing the shrine is a small trade-off for safety.

It is our plan tomorrow to be up at the crack of dawn, dressed, fed, packed and checked out of our rooms by 7:10 AM. The Tibet Guest House will store our luggage while we are gone and we have all been encouraged to pack light for our side trip. We should be able to get to the airport in the hotel vans before the curfew takes affect.

The strike/bandha is in effect nationwide so we are not expecting to find Pokhara as delightfully welcoming as it might be at another time. Pokhara is a lakeside resort town with panoramic views of the Annapurna mountain range. It is popular with Israelis and hippies who never went home. We plan to visit the Tibetan Refugee Camp at Tashi Pakheil in order to observe the shamanic work being done by three powerful Tibetan shamans who live there. The grandfather shaman Pau Wang Chuk has been a shamanic practitioner since he was twelve and he is now 85ish. As a Living Treasure of Michael Harner's Foundation for Shamanic Studies, Wang Chuk receives $250 annually to help his shamanic practice. Bel and Somendra Thapa are Magar shamans. The Magars are one of the oldest known tribes in Nepal. We should also be able to shop the bazaar along the shores of Lake Phewa, hike to the Peace Pagoda, go horseback riding or enjoy the pleasures of the world famous Fulbari Resort and Spa. Larry has opted to stay at the Glacier Hotel rather than the Fulbari because the resort's management is in flux. The last time Larry stayed there the group experienced leaky roofs, mold in the rooms and rancid food. The spa, however, has an elaborate website describing its services and I am preparing to indulge in their Secret Yarchagumba Himalayan Facial, Ancient Thai Massage followed by a luxurious Floral Jacuzzi during which you dip yourself in a warm bath filled with fresh flower petals while sipping their special tea. I'll leave the horseback riding to Denise!

Several members of our group are intentionally not watching the news. They feel the media sensationalizes everything and they simply don't want to give the media power. But I feel that during this turbulent time, I want to know what is going on. This is history in the making.

In surfing the television channels I have come across the Nepali version of MTV. Their videos are very entertaining and prove that music spans the language barriers. For instance, the tall skinny suitor standing in a rice paddy with an umbrella hat on his head is obviously unwelcome in the upper class walled compound of the hip swiveling vixen for whom he pines.

The palace-imposed curfew is being defied all over Kathmandu. There are stories of shots being fired in the air and rounds of tear gas shells being thrown into crowds in an attempt to disperse them. There have been injuries and arrests. We heard that a protestor has been shot dead in Pokhara when the army opened fire on the demonstrators.

Our itinerary has, obviously, been affected by our inability to move about and the inability of Larry's staff to get to us. We missed visiting Gokarna where there is a forest and game preserve that was once the private hunting grounds of the king of Nepal.

We had been scheduled for a day trip to Dakshinkali in a valley south of Kathmandu where there is a shrine to Kali of the South. Legend has it that there was a cholera epidemic in the 1300's, and people were dying in large numbers. So the local Hindus decided to make a sacrifice to appease Kali, the goddess of death and destruction. They built a temple over the stream. They then sacrificed a large number of water buffalo, letting the blood flow into the stream, and lo and behold the cholera epidemic stopped. Seeing the cause and effect, they decided to keep on sacrificing animals at this place to keep everyone healthy. Chickens are the chosen sacrifices these days and after they are ritually beheaded, the body of the bird is given back to the family and they take it onto a hillside to cook it up for a picnic lunch.

We would also have visited the Pharphing Monastery and the Guru Rinpoche Enlightenment Cave where Guru Rinpoche did a two-year meditation, paving the way for Tibet's receptivity to the teachings of the Buddha.

I will have to absorb these experiences vicariously from guidebooks, glossy coffee table books or the photographs of others…or, perhaps, just perhaps, wait for another visit to Nepal at another time.

Aama was able to get to us today and we set up a room-to-room healing schedule. The group was invited to observe the in-room healings. When everyone got to Room 304 I sat in front of Aama and explained that I have pain in my back that I assume is a pinched nerve. It has been chronic for a very long time. Aama touched my forehead, threw some rice and began her incantation "Shep Se Te Nee…" while counting on her fingers. She reached around me and placed her hand directly on the place that bothers me. She spoke some mantras and then told me to use the mustard oil that she had given me for my knees on my back as well. I was grateful for the healing. Each time another physical issue is dealt with, I feel like a layer of the onion has been peeled away and I will eventually emerge whole and strong.

We finished our day of confinement with dinner in the hotel restaurant, which, I discovered, actually has a name. It is called the Nurbu Restaurant. Jeff had discovered Tagliatelli Verde which is a close relative of Chicken (or Shrimp) Alfredo and I copycatted his order.

My nightly email is a sign-off for a few days as I am unsure of the availability of Internet access in Pokhara. The Dark Lady who oversees the cyber room at the Tibet Guest House glides from computer to computer, fixing errors and making sure nobody gets away without paying the posted fees.

She has a melancholy cloud around her and she seems annoyed that anyone is actually using the computers.

# CHAPTER 15
## April 9, 2006 SUNDAY
## BUDDHA AIR TO POKHARA, MIGMAR & YESHI

I still don't have a clock so I just begin my day when the sun comes up. I've convinced myself that this is my hedge against jet lag. I just won't let my body know what time it is. But today was different. I had to be ready to go by 7:10, so I slept fitfully and was afraid I would oversleep. The logical remedy was not to sleep.

At a little after 7 AM we jammed into two hotel vans and headed for the airport with the intention of getting there before the daily curfew began. Ram and Pramod were walking to meet us from the other direction.

The city is on edge. People were bustling around trying to get their daily activities accomplished before the curfew began and police and army personnel are on every street corner.

Near the airport gate we stopped and waited for Ram and Pramod. Larry was nervously checking his watch and we were holding our breath. The curfew hour was approaching, so the van driver agreed to head towards Pramod's neighborhood in hopes that we would find them. All of us spotted the pair at the same moment and there was a great sigh of relief. Quickly the van turned back to the airport and deposited us all at the terminal.

Buddha Air had not yet opened, so we left our luggage in an office and went to hang out in the airport restaurant. The dining tables and chairs were tired and the faded yellow walls needed paint, but it was acceptably clean and some of the group ordered coffee and toast. And we waited…and I dozed. Everyone has become used to the fact that I doze often and anywhere.

Eventually the appropriate counters opened and we were able to proceed through security. Susan wears a hand-hammered silver goddess pendant and the goddess holds a half moon in one hand. The security lady patted Susan down quite extensively and cut her hand on Susan's half moon. It actually drew blood! We were surprised the security lady allowed her to keep the pendant. Both Larry and Jeff were frisked and Larry was fuming that he "had been handled". Jeff took it in stride.

From the bus we could see the modern brick terminal reserved for the king's comings and goings. Whenever the king or a visiting head of state arrives at Kathmandu's Tribhuvan Airport, five teenage girls known as the Pancha Kumari welcome the dignitaries by placing flower garlands around their necks. Across the tarmac our Beechcraft 1900D nineteen-seat prop plane waited. The dozen or so steps up the staircase to the door had a sign that said "One Person at a Time". I wonder what would happen if two people ascended at once. Would the plane roll over on its side? There was a single row of seats on each side of a narrow aisle. We could look straight down the aisle into the cockpit. Our stewardess, dressed in jeans and a red tee shirt and chewing gum, offered us cotton for our ears and a hard candy for the pressure. After we were air born she came down the aisle with a liter bottle of Pepsi, which she offered in small paper cups. As we rose over the Kathmandu Valley we were able to see terraced farmland, small villages and the magnificent Himalayas beyond.

I have seen photographs of the Himalayas all my life, but I cannot explain how breath-taking the experience of seeing the snow-covered peaks with my own eyes was. The flight from Kathmandu to Pokhara was less than 30 minutes.

*Annapurna range of the Himalayas*
*(Taken by Sue Melanson)*

Pokhara is much more tropical than Kathmandu and as we descended we could see deep green lakes, a huge waterfall, steep jungle-covered mountains and, beyond, the Annapurna range of the Himalayans. As we dropped lower we observed that there was no vehicular traffic anywhere. There were a couple of black plumes of smoke and a single fire engine speeding towards them.

In order to get to the Glacier Hotel we had to ride in a police van with a military driver and a second uniformed guard carrying a sub machine gun. Several girls from another tour group were already in the back seat of the van and Pramod convinced them that another van was leaving immediately and they would do better in that van. The girls scrambled out and we filled the van. Denise asked Pramod how he knew there was another van. He winked and said, "Oh, is there another van?"

Pokhara seemed to be locked down just as tight as Kathmandu. No vehicles. No shops opened. No people on the streets. Our police van entered the gates of the Glacier Hotel and we all piled out.

*Glacier Hotel*

The hotel is within a walled compound that also includes a lush garden and the Romeo Restaurant, which is a separate building opening straight onto the sidewalk. Our host greeted us. He was a charming man, smiling and bowing, wearing a white panama suit and a goodly dollop of Brill Cream in his hair. I think he is going for a Mohawk look but his black hair was only long enough to create a wind-row.

While we settled in our rooms, Larry and Sarah set out on foot to try to find Migmar, our translator. Migmar and her husband, Yeshi, own the Kijimuna Tibetan Shop in the lakeside bazaar.

Denise and I were very pleased with our comfortable room. Larry told us that our belongings are not as safe in hotels in Pokhara as they had been in the Tibet Guest House and we should watch what we left around. Our room has a large locking cabinet, which instantly made us feel safe. The cabinet did not, however, lock efficiently, but the appearance of safety was there.

We gathered in the garden where Burt was attempting to educate Ram on the English names for various flowers. Ram was nodding his head politely and held his pen over a notepad just in case Burt said something important. The pen wasn't moving. A couple of geckos scurried across the grass and peered at us from a Hibiscus bush. We ordered cold drinks (I really miss ice!) and we basked in the sun waiting for Larry and Sarah to come back.

When Larry and Sarah returned we learned that King Gyanendra and his queen are staying at the Ratna Mandir Royal Palace, which is right across the street from our hotel. There is a strong military presence in Pokhara and the four-day strike has been extended indefinitely. The curfew, however has been eased up and now seems to apply to Nepalis only. Westerners can move about undisturbed. While Larry and Sarah were walking a Nepali accountant came up and asked to walk with them. If they were stopped he was going to say that he was their interpreter. He was desperate to get to his office and was very grateful for the escort. Migmar and Yeshi were in their shop and they planned to join us for dinner.

Larry was trying to decide the best plan of action, taking into consideration all the new information he and Sarah had gleaned. He asked us to meet on the balcony at our usual four o'clock meeting hour.

Denise and I lay on our beds watching the overhead fan revolve and wondering whether we had been given pillows or sandbags for our heads. We lay there just talking about "stuff". With Denise "stuff" is not superfluous fluff. She has skills and gifts for healing and understanding people that far surpass the average Joe. I was blessed and honored to be taken into her confidence and to hear about the many aspects and anecdotes that are Denise. Likewise, I opened up to her and we established a unique bond and understanding. Before we leave Pokhara she will teach me a Kung Fu stance that will help strengthen my legs and my lower back. She is also making me think about my career as a reporter at home. With great compassion and humor, Denise identified a characteristic in me that I had heretofore ignored. I am a gossip! Being a reporter requires this instinct. That's how stories begin...a tip, a rumor...gossip. Then a good reporter goes in after the facts to substantiate the story...unless you work for the tabloids. I have developed that trait...but to what end. I don't think I like being a gossip. Do I even like being a reporter?

At four everyone met on the balcony. Without transportation of any kind, there will be only one way to get to the Tibetan Refugee Camp at Tarshi Palkhiel. We will have to walk. Larry has decided that we can do the seven-mile trek very early in the morning but everyone has to understand that if we get out there and someone's legs give out, there is no taxi to hail or option of any sort to get back to the hotel. I very much want to visit Tarshi Palkhiel and have the opportunity to observe the shamans that practice there, especially Pau Wang Chuk. I weighed the benefits of the excursion against the reality that I was not in shape to do a 15-mile round trip hike. The reality won out and I quietly announced that I would not be making the trek. Larry was relieved, but Susan burst into tears. She was upset that the group would be separated. Susan and I stepped into my room and I explained to Susan that it is okay. This was the way it is supposed to be. I also suspect that Erica and Sarah are thinking about staying behind. The Australians are so much into their own world that it is hard to figure out what they are thinking, but June's color is not good and she has visibly lost weight since we came to Nepal. I had heard that she does triathlons (a rumor...gossip), but she looks frail to me. I wonder if she can make the trek.

And so the plan is set. The group will rise at 5 AM and hike to Tarshi Palkhiel. All but me! I will get to sleep in, enjoy a leisurely breakfast and soak up the amazing view of Machhapuchhre, the Fishtail Mountain, from the roof of the hotel. I will establish my own mini-adventure tomorrow.

We met Migmar and Yeshi at the Moon Dance Restaurant just down the street from the hotel. Moon Dance is exactly what I envisioned exotic Nepal to offer to the adventurous world-travelers of the 1960's. It is a high-ceiling warehouse creatively decorated with black canvas ceiling panels, yellow stucco walls, deep cushioned wicker chairs that invite patrons to sit and lounge and a pool table loft. The maitre'd knows Larry and was thrilled to welcome us. You can order pizza with real Mozzarella cheese at Moon Dance, and they have an ample supply of beer. The kitchen communicates with the wait staff by setting off an electronic birdcall when an order is ready. We ate hearty tonight, and drank more than a few Tiger Beers. Migmar and Yeshi became part of our growing Nepali family.

*Migmar and Yeshi Lama*
(Taken by Sue Melanson)

Migmar is a tiny lady with a broad smile and sensitivity for everything and everyone around her. She very much wants us to understand the plight of the Tibetans in Nepal. Prior to the Maoist (Chinese Communist) military invasion of Tibet in 1959, the Dalai Lama acted as the religious and secular leader of Tibet. His Holiness was forced by the Chinese army to flee from his home at the Norbulingka Summer Palace in Lhasa to Dharamsala in Northern India. Many Tibetans fled with him to India or to Nepal. Many died en route. The settlement at Tarshi Palkhiel was established in 1962. The first thing the refugees needed was basic food and shelter, healthcare to cope with widespread illness brought on by being exposed to the new tropical climate, as well as an education system designed to preserve the Tibetan culture and religion. Today every family has a house, and nearly every child between the ages of five and thirteen attends the settlement school. The school is a single-story building with ten classrooms and a library. Tibetan children from the settlement and from the higher Himalayas receive instruction there. The children from remote areas live with orphans in an orphanage that Migmar referred to as a "boarding house". It can accommodate a "family" of sixty children at a time. Often non-Tibetans from the surrounding communities will pay to have their children educated at Tarshi Palkhiel. The settlement also has a home for the elderly who have lost their families, a clinic and a monastery. A handicraft center provides jobs but the main source of income is their carpet factories. They are known for the consistently high-quality carpets they produce. But, Migmar pointed out, "We are a disenfranchised people. We have no country." Since there is no longer a Tibet, they are not considered Tibetans. Yet they are not Nepalis either. If they were to apply for Nepali citizenship they would be turning their backs on their true heritage and accepting an identity, not as Tibetans but as second-class Nepali citizens. "Free Tibet" tee shirts that are often seen in the United States are frowned on in Nepal. I had noticed that Shaym Panchit, the little tee shirt entrepreneur in Kathmandu, is selling the shirts, but they are not prominently displayed.

I asked Migmar about the fate of the Norbulingka Summer Palace in Lhasa. With tears in her eyes she said, "It stands empty."

After dinner we strolled back to the Glacier Hotel, breathing the thick tropical night air that brings forth floral fragrances that aren't there in the daytime. The stone palace barracks flank the street to the right, and small storefronts getting ready to close for the evening lined the street to our left. We knew army watchers were in the shadows and occasionally we set off a motion-sensor light, but all in all Pokhara seemed peaceful. We walked around the three-foot coil of barbed wire that is stretched across the street near the palace gate and back to the hotel compound.

Denise and I showered, climbed into bed and talked long into the night. I like having a roommate!

# CHAPTER 16
## April 10, 2006 MONDAY
## POKHARA'S GLACIER HOTEL AND MOON DANCE

At 5 AM the telephone range. I assumed it was a wake-up call for Denise, so I just rolled over. Denise lifted the receiver, hung up and also rolled over. It rang again. This time she actually said "Hello". It was Larry. He was canceling the hike to Tarshi Palkhiel. He had decided it was too dangerous. So we both rolled over and went back to sleep.

Hours later we were getting dressed when we heard Erica and Susan singing. We looked out the window and discovered that they were serenading a small family of Water Buffalo wandering below our windows. We chimed in and the unfamiliar strains of "Oh, What A Beautiful Morning" made the buffs move along more quickly.

*Water Buffalo*
*(Taken by Sue Melanson)*

Erica, the most creative in our band, had dreamed up a scheme whereby we could all make enough money to pay for our trip AND maybe a second trip at a less politically unstable time. She thought we could put our heads together and create a shamanic board game. Erica's board game idea was brilliant. The game would be formatted around the mandala of the

Kathmandu Valley. It would be multi-dimensional, perhaps lending itself to becoming a video game. There would be a Cosmos laid out with Upper World, Lower World and Middle World full of deities, legends and anecdotes. The players would have a chance to interact with Shiva, Brahma and Vishnu, Buddhas and their Taras, Mother Goddesses, the youthful Kumari, the Bon Jankrit, various historical Rinpoches, the Nagas, Yama the Lord of Death, etc. etc. and at any time you might draw that capricious "Bad Days and Planets" card. The game would also have a level of tourism just to make it interesting: restaurants, shops, historical monuments, stupas, shrines and temples. Stumbling blocks could involve "Drank bad water. Go to the Cipro Store."; "Need to exchange Travelers Checks. Miss a turn."; "Baggage overweight. Pay 500 rupees."; "Score some Yarchagumba. Go play in the garden."; "Begin Again. Ask Ganesh for blessings." The ideas were plentiful but we never got focused enough to write it all down.

We had seen a coffee house just a few doors away and, by lunchtime, the lure of real coffee was strong, but we opted to eat in the hotel restaurant. It had a concrete floor, galvanized metal roof, tie-dyed tablecloths and well-worn wicker seating – not comfortable, welcoming worn, but rickety, in-need-of-repair worn. The waiters were slow to assist us and it was hard to tell who worked there. Larry suggested pushing some of the tables together and all of a sudden we were being given attention – by the manager. He had a fit about the idea of moving the tables, and that was the end of Dr. Larry and the Romeo Restaurant. We ended up at the Monsoon Restaurant two doors away.

The Monsoon was not very much of an upgrade from the Romeo Restaurant, but they allowed us to put the tables together. There was only one other couple in the restaurant and they were sitting gazing at the lake and enjoying a cigarette, which they shared. Erica was the first to notice the smell. "Smells like college." Yes, indeed, the shared cigarette was a joint. Now that's what I call second hand smoke!

Erica is always the one to find levity in a situation. She asked Larry what event on his many pilgrimages to Nepal made him the most nervous. She was trying to smooth over the fact that the current "event" was undoubtedly getting a little scary. Larry sat back and thought. He then related how a former adventurer named Dr. Judy had tried to French kiss a cobra...that made him nervous.

Later in the afternoon, Jeff suggested we take advantage of our proximity to the king and do some journeywork. We might actually be able to influence some positive change in the atmosphere. June and Burt were outraged. They had made no bones about letting us know how they felt about the king. They hated him and June had gone so far as to suggest someone should kill him. The only drums we had were theirs and we hoped they might put their personal avarice aside to, at the very least, drum for the rest of us. This, however, never happened. They retreated to their room and were not seen for the rest of the afternoon.

It was not our intent to heal the king; it was to diffuse the very volatile political situation. The journey was intended to bring more far-reaching results for the good of the kingdom...for the good of mankind. We set our intent and those of us with rattles began the percussive beginning of our non-ordinary reality journey.

Way in the distance, around the summit of the mountain on which the World Peace Pagoda stands, two huge Golden Eagles began to soar. One flap of their mighty wings would set them into a long slow glide, assisted by mountain thermals.

*JOURNEY:*

The Golden Eagles were hovering in ordinary reality but they transferred into non-ordinary reality as my journey began and they were joined by familiar Bald Eagles streaming red, white and blue banners behind them.

My journey began in front of the Ajima Temple hearing again the story of the goddess who was taught a lesson in compassion by Buddha when he hid her youngest child under a basket so she would feel what other parents feel who have lost children because of Ajima. The lesson was compassion and the king was the intended recipient of the lesson.

I was reminded of the evening of 9/11. My friend, Pat and I drummed for hours that evening and it felt like I was stroking a huge injured cat. The magnitude of the situation was beyond comprehension and all I could do was offer a soothing touch, as if stroking the universe. I think I would have felt very helpless had I not had this basic tool of shamanism   Today felt much the same.

I was raised in a patriotic home. Both of my parents were US Navy officers during WW II. I always came to attention and sang the "Star Spangled Banner" with pride, and often with tears in my eyes. I was taught to be a proud American, and despite troubled times, I still am.

I was shown a memory, a piece of my own history, in order to remind me of the emotion of the times. It was 1968 and I was at the Democratic Convention in Chicago. I felt fear and apprehension. I felt outrage and frustration at the war in Vietnam. And I felt a passion deep in my soul that I could make a difference. My journeys are often set against significant musical backgrounds. The Moody Blues came into my journey singing:

> *I remember the taste of the vintage wine*
> *From '63 through to '69*
> *And I'm proud of the things we believed in then*
> *If I had the chance I'd go around again*
> *Oh I tell you*
> *We were young and free*
> *Oh I'll tell you*
> *'Cause I was there you see*

My spirit guides kept me hanging around Mayor Daly's city for awhile just to be sure I got a good taste of what it felt to be me in 1968. The peace dove on McCarthy's campaign pins meant something.

Next I found myself in the courtyard of the monastery next to the Chinea Lama's house and naked nymphs were dancing around the huge prayer wheel, making it spin with great speed. They were lighthearted creatures spilling mirth and happiness everywhere they went, as in "Peter Pan" they could sprinkle Fairy Dust to ignite the magic of the universe.

Then I was guided to the stupa where Mujiba had encountered the cockroach. And there it was again peering out of the sacred statuary. Only this time it had on a tuxedo and was carrying a little cane. It did a few dance steps and then broke into a full-fledged tap-dancing routine to an oriental version of "Puttin' on the Ritz". It then did a flick of its multiple insect wrists and turned into a butterfly with red/white/blue wings. It flew straight at my face whispering, "Don't miss the message." I gathered that it was showing me a trick of metamorphosis, similar to what both Nepal and the United States are going through right now. Growing pains! Transformation! Another message came fast on the heels of the first: "Don't get bogged down in expectation". The outcome will be as it is supposed to be. Thy will be done."

The rattles signaled a callback and I returned to the balcony of the Glacier Hotel. The Golden Eagles were no longer visible across the lake.

As I shared my journey, I was overcome with a sense of patriotism. I was proud to be an American. And I was equally proud to be a part of Nepal.

Larry was gauging the situation outside the hotel compound walls and he decided we would be able to walk to Migmar's shop before dinner, deliver the spirit gifts we had all brought for the Tibetan shamans -- Migmar would have to deliver them -- and stop at Moon Dance for dinner on our way back. We all wanted to see Migmar's shop, but the walk to the lakeside bazaar was not a casual stroll. We moved right along, noting the other shops along the way but not stopping. We were aware of military presence both visible and concealed. There was a raw energy in the air that could explode at any moment.

*Pokhara begins to heat up*
(Taken by Sue Melanson)

We arrived at the shop just after they had closed, but Larry hailed Migmar and Yeshi and they were more than happy to open up for us. The strike and curfew had been a difficult financial loss for them.

There were glass cabinets of jewelry; statuary on shelves, both metallic and wooden; singing bowls of all sizes; hand-held prayer wheels; funky fur trimmed hats; prayer flags; wall hangings; images of deities; incense; bells, changs (finger bells that look something like castinets) and gongs.

I discovered a fascinating artifact in a cabinet. It was a silver-trimmed Thighbone Trumpet. It is called a "staggling" if it is made of tiger bone or a "kangling" if it is made of human bone. Both are ritual instruments used in sacred ceremony. These trumpets are decorated and fitted with a mouth-piece. Tibetan Buddhist's believe that they harness the energy of the wind as they blow the trumpets, warning spirits of the impending ceremony. The human bone is also intended to remind both the player and listener of his own impermanent existence. They make strange, penetrating, otherworldly sounds. Larry explained that the piece was undoubtedly very expensive, but beyond that he doubted we would be able to get such an item through customs. I picked it up and looked it over. I will probably never have the experince of handling such an item again. It had a strange energy to it – a sad female energy, as if the woman had died in childbirth.

While we browsed we piled our spirit gifts on the counter for the Tibetan shamans. It was very frustrating to be leaving these special gifts for unseen faces. I had brought maple syrup from our own sugar bush and a bag of our private label pancake mix.

I went back several times to look at a particular set of earrings, but Migmar and Yeshi were swamped with the in-process purchases of my comrades.

Jeff asked to see a silver sculpture of Shiva and Parvoti in an embrace. When Yeshi lifted the statue down the two figures came apart as they were designed to do. And there they lay in anatomically correct detail having been extracted from their sexual union. The ultimate coitus interuptus! Once Jeff saw the detail of the piece he bought it there and then, and we all wished we had been the ones to discover its interactive secret.

Outside the tension was growing. A truck of army personnel drove by in the direction of a crowd forming at the opposite end of the street. Several shopkeepers lowered their shop fronts in case rioting broke out. The possibility seemed imminent. Our shopping divas were so focused on their discoveries that Sarah and Larry's urging to speed up the shopping spree fell on deaf ears. June and Burt were the first ones to bolt. On foot and alone they headed back to the hotel. The demonstrators at the end of the street were increasing in numbers and noise. After the last credit card transaction was processed, we headed back to the hotel. Once underway we felt more confident and decided to stop at Moon Dance for dinner as planned. Any clashes between military and civilians were bound to happen at the far end of the lakeside bazaar.

The fact that the king is in Pokhara will probably mean that the violence we had seen in Kathmandu will begin here, so we will cut our visit short and will fly back tomorrow. As Larry said, we are one step closer to getting out of the country if we have to from Kathmandu.

The news is reporting garbage piling up in the streets of Kathmandu as sanitation workers cannot collect it due to the strike and curfew.

# CHAPTER 17
## April 11, 2006 TUESDAY
## RETURN TO KATHMANDU FROM POKHARA

Breakfast was served in the garden where Migmar and Yeshi joined us. The garden scenario may have been because the Glacier Hotel felt badly about Larry's nasty encounter with their restaurant staff. Or it may have been because it was too dangerous to eat in the restaurant that opened onto the street. The news headlines are calling the situation in Pokhara "fluid, dangerous and precipitative".

*Breakfast in the Glacier Hotel garden*
(Taken by Sue Melanson)

We gathered our luggage and said our goodbyes to Migmar. She gave each of us a golden katag (prayer scarf) as we parted.

*Migmar and Sue Melanson*
(Taken by Mujiba Cabugos)

Before leaving we climbed to the roof of the hotel to take on last picture of Machhupuchare, the "Fish Tail" mountain.

Machhupuchare, the "Fish Tail" mountain
(Taken by Sue Melanson)

This time we were able to get to the airport by hotel van. On the way we observed minimal vehicular traffic and the same closed shops we had seen everywhere coming in.

Buddha Air transported us back to Kathmandu and the vans from the Tibet Guest House took us to our home away from home. The hotel was not expecting us back for several days so our previous rooms were unavailable for most of us. There are several groups of trekkers stranded there and they have been unable to move to their next destination. I ended up in Room 207 directly above the restaurant. Susan is across the hall in an even less desirable situation. She has to turn the water on at the wall to make her toilet flush and she woke up face to face with a "tick" in her bed. I didn't want to be an alarmist and utter the dread words "bed bug", but I think all of us were thinking it. My room is clean and has an overhead fan, which provides both air circulation and "white noise". The bathroom has two drawbacks. First, there is a window beside the bathtub with a curtain. The bathtub is narrow and fitted with a shower curtain. This means that between the window curtain and the shower curtain, showering is a battle between the two curtains and my soapy body. Second, there is a ventilation transom above the vanity that opens directly into the hotel hallway.

The hotel offers a laundry service, but Larry has indicated that he does not think they do a very good job. He recommended taking our laundry to a place he uses. Unfortunately we have been unable to get to Larry's laundry and my "to do" pile is getting bigger. I had picked up an elegant little container of bubble bath at the Amari Hotel in Bangkok and I decided it was time to turn it into laundry detergent. I had brought more than enough panties from home, but I am realizing that the weight I had lost before the trip combined with what I have apparently lost since we arrived in Nepal, is creating an interesting phenomena. Sometimes, if I turn quickly, my over-sized underwear does not turn with me and creates a pseudo-wedgey. About a year ago my friends and I participated in a Panty Chain Letter. My friend Ellen's daughter had sent me a particularly elegant pair in a leopard skin print that I wear every time I need a little extra spunk (giving a presentation, meeting new people, etc.). It's my under cover wear secret weapon! I have decided that all but the leopard skin can be discarded when I leave in order to provide more packing room.

Aama came to the hotel to do healings for us and provide a training opportunity for the group. I expected to give her the kurta today, but, when it came time, Sarah told Mujiba and I that she had already given it to her when they were alone. So much for the gift being from all three of us! I feel ripped off and cheated. Sarah had no right to do it this way. She claims that she was so excited that she couldn't help herself and just HAD to give it to Aama the instant she saw her. It must never have occurred to her that Mujiba and I felt the same way.

Dinner came around and I went looking for the group but did not find them. It was the first case of what happens when the buddy system has not provided for everyone. The group had left for dinner without me. Even the Mother Hen did not notice that I was missing. I ate alone in the restaurant and ordered apple fritters for dessert, which were totally unappealing and unable to assuage my hurt feelings that the group had departed without me.

The uncertainty of the entire situation here is wearing on everyone, we are emotionally exhausted, and there is bickering amongst our temporary little family. It occurred to me to bale out and ask Larry to put me on a plane for home as soon as possible, but I need to exercise patience and wisdom. It is more prudent to hang in here, experience the initiation I came for, and return home with the group. It will be safer than flying stand-by alone. I also recognize that there is a degree of homesickness that may be skewing my perspective.

Carin is a shamanic healer in Massachusetts who came to Nepal with Larry in 2002. She sent me an email while we were in Pokhara that I only picked up tonight. It had a good message for me. Carin wrote: "I have been working a lot these days with my guides about ways to stay present, full and wholehearted in the face of adversity and challenge. How do I choose to BE and what, if anything, is there to DO to support the return of balance? These are wonderful teachings and I hope they can be of service to you during these stirred up times in Nepal."

Larry has told us that if everything falls apart, we will be leaving. I am not unpacking this time. Living out of my suitcase makes getting out quickly more of a possibility. If, perchance, we are unable to do the initiation during Thursday's Full Moon, Larry has suggested that we all meet at his home in California on Memorial Day Weekend. Aama will be there for healings and can do the initiation. I have been planning that my final trip across the world to home will be the last plane trip I ever take, but if Plan B is necessary I will certainly make the effort to be there.

As night fell over Kathmandu, I became aware of another drawback to Room 207. June and Burt must have been two floors directly above me and they like to end their days drumming. Not peaceful, heartbeat drumming, but erratic, uncontrolled noise. Even the barking dog next door shut up.

# CHAPTER 18
## April 12, 2006 WEDNESDAY
## US EMBASSY ASKS AMERICANS TO EVALUATE THEIR PERSONAL SECURITY POSTURE

Today we began with a meeting in the garden and our interpreters filled us in on the latest news. And the news is significant.

The US Embassy has given permission for their affiliated family members and non-emergency personnel to depart Nepal and have advised Americans in the country to evaluate their personal security posture and consider whether it is appropriate to remain in Nepal. Anti-monarchy protests continue and the king is using "shoot to kill" curfews to thwart the demonstrations. Demonstrators are defying the curfews. Thousands have been arrested, including thirty journalists. I was deliberate when I left any identification at home affiliating me with my newspaper. Here the little *Sacopee Valley Citizen* might as well be the *New York Times*. Four people have been killed since the strike and curfew began April 6. Communication by mobile phone has been cut off and the king has threatened to cut off telephone communication and the Internet. The Maoist insurgency is becoming very active and the United States Department of State has declared the Communist Party of Nepal (the Maoists) to be a "specifically designated terrorist organization". The Maoists have pledged specific action against U.S. citizens in areas where they are active.

The king has returned to the city and everyone is waiting. Friday is the Nepali New Year and he is expected to address the people at that time.

Every day we wait to hear if there will be a curfew. There is very little lead-time before the monarchy decides to impose curfew or lift it. Today they lifted the curfew and the shops are open. The strike, however, continues and this affects transportation. Jigme comes to us from Bouddhanath by bicycle. Sano Ram lives near Swayambhu and he walks to the Tibet Guest House. Pramod and Ram walk, when they can, from Pramod's neighborhood near Bouddhanath. We don't know when Aama will be able to get to us again.

Larry is keeping a close eye on the political situation and has a network of people all over the city. For the moment he has decided to stay, but that could change quickly if things deteriorate. We have, quite literally, put our lives in his hands.

But this morning we were able to shop.

During the past few days I have been able to duck across the alley to Shaym Pandit's tee shirt shop. He embroiders tee shirts on his sewing machine and was able to transfer the logo taken from my business card for our High Acres Maple Syrup directly onto a tee shirt. Jeff ordered tee shirts for his entire running team and had their logo custom embroidered. And these custom tee shirts cost less than $10 US each. In addition to the High Acres tee shirt (which I intend to give to Art), I had Shaym make three for me: an intricately detailed Ganesh tee shirt, a navy blue "Nepal" tee shirt and one with "Kathmandu" on it. I am having one with three fuzzy yaks on it that says "Yak Yak Yak" for my son-in-law-to-be, and a Mount Everest shirt for my brother. I swung by Shaym's to pick up a white embroidered gauze shirt he had made for me for tomorrow's initiation.

A little girl on the street was selling sets of three nested change purses. In perfect English she explained to me that the big one is for "folding money", the middle one is for "metal money", and the third one is for "tokens". I asked what she meant by tokens. Transportation tokens? "No", she replied, "tokens for slot machines." I guess we Westerners have a perceptual reputation. I bought several sets from her for $1 US each.

There is a corner shop we have all visited. A father and son keep the place open even in the face of everything that is going on. Neither speaks very good English but they know who we are and will send for their "brother", who always appears in a baseball cap with a credit card machine in hand. He speaks perfect English and even understands our humor. I am not a shopper, but I want to bring the perfect gift home to my special people. Under normal circumstances I would poke and think and come back and try other shops, but our experience of having erratic access to stores made me more capricious and suddenly this little shop on the corner had something for everyone. There was a rose quartz crystal for this one, and earrings for that one, and a silver pendant for myself. Joahnna asked for a pebble and the perfect pebble was right in front of me. The proprietor's "brother" called it "sun stone" but I think it might be jasper. They carefully wrapped each object in little fabric drawstring presentation bags. After I had made all my selections I whipped out my trusty credit card and the "brother" called in the total. And we waited. After an excruciating period of time he told me the card had been rejected. I was furious and mortified all at once. My fellow travelers said I should have notified the credit card company so they know they may see charges from Nepal. I knew I had the cash back at the hotel and told them I would be right back. These fellows were not ones to easily let a "live one" walk away, so they sent the young boy back to the hotel with me, clutching my bag of goodies in his hand. He waited by the front desk while I fetched the cash and he handed me my purchases with a lot of bowing and Namaste-ing. My $89 US purchase may have made the day for the shop.

Our group had a luncheon date at Gauri's Thangka shop. The repast was momos (both meat and vegetarian), pickle and fried potatoes. We looked over Gauri's wares and Larry lost an eye to a very unusual Thangka that depicted Durga on her Tiger assisted by a Bon Jankrit fighting off an army of demons. Larry's house is full of Thangkas, but he just had to take this one too. Larry and Carol even have a Thangka mounted on the ceiling over their bed.

It was 2 o'clock when we left Gauri's. At home we always have coffee at 2. It is a habit Art brought home from his years as an oil tanker captain. But here good coffee is unknown. Mostly it is instant, but that could be because the restaurants have been having trouble getting supplies with the strike and curfew. I found myself staring at my toenail polish and suddenly realizing that my toes, that I had had meticulously pedicured before the trip, were Dunkin Donuts pink. Am I addicted to coffee? I think I am!

After leaving Gauri's I went across the street to pick up my drum. The cover that had been custom made was exquisitely done in brocade with heavy gold and silver beading on one side and blue/green tapestry on the other.

Most of us had shaman drums (dhyandros) made for us. The two-sided goatskin drum is stretched over a frame of hazel wood and played with a curved vine-like drumstick. When the drums were made, a sacred Rudraksya seed and a Ridha seed as well as a copper coin were placed inside the drum. The artists at Gauri's Thangka shop painted them.

*Shaman drum painted by Thangka artists*
(Taken by Sue Melanson)

On one side, the male side of the drum, is the trident of Shiva flanked by the moon and sun representing the powers of light and darkness. A pair of bow and arrows point left and right to guard against bad spirits. White dots around the edge represent the stars and planets. On the other side, the female side of the drum, is a lotus flower. Brahma, the Creator of the Universe, was born in the lotus flower. The handle is a carved wooden phurba, which is a three sided ritual dagger often used in extraction work. When we beat the dhyandro we are calling the spirits.

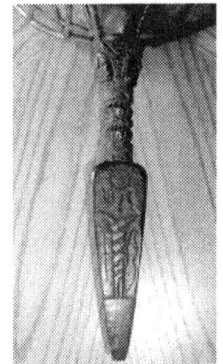

*Phurba handle of the drum*
(Taken by Sue Melanson)

There was a woman in the drum-cover shop from Bristol, Vermont. She had come to Nepal as a Peace Corps worker in the 1970's and never left. The Peace Corps, however, suspended operations in Nepal in 2004.

A group of Western tourists, none that we know, staged a demonstration of their own yesterday carrying a sign saying, "End the curfew". It was a stupid and dangerous chance they took and all nine were arrested. We are being very careful to observe the curfews and stay away from crowds. It has required a lot of creative planning on Larry's part.

This afternoon we met on the roof so Sano Ram could teach us what we need to know for tomorrow's initiation.

We began by talking about mantras. The meaning of the initiation mantra Sano Ram uses is as follows:

> We ask for blessings.
> We are here to respect you.
> We are here in costume. Please help us.
> We are here in your shrine.
> We want you to be happy with us
> and help us with our work.

This is Sano Ram's personal mantra. Everyone has their own mantra for different purposes. You receive your mantra in a dream or a journey…a gift given from guru to a disciple. A "mantra" is a sacred sound. A "yantra" is a sacred design, typically a mandala that is worshipped visually. A "tantra" is a sacred motion or movement.

Sano Ram taught us the shaman dance. This dance is Sano Ram's forte…his claim to fame. When the Bon Jankrit (yeti) kidnapped Sano Ram as a child, he was taught shamanism and they taught him to dance. His agility and energy is enhanced when he is doing sacred work and he can leap and jump higher and farther than just about anyone. The purpose of dancing is to carry the power of the deities in our bodies.

Larry reviewed the initiation day events. The pilgrimage we will be embarking on is a means for initiating new shamans as well as the renewal of experienced shamans. The difference between an individual pilgrimage whereby the person is seeking personal healing, is that shamans hope to acquire power to be used in healings in their own communities. First, we will set out for a shrine to gain power to do healing. At the shrine we will do ritual, make offerings, which, typically, might include flowers, flour, soul flowers, red ochre, or rice. We don't have access to any of this so we may offer a few rupees and ask for healing power. We will do the Shaman Dance which is a spiritual soul calling. Traditionally, we would then weave titi paati (Mugwort in the US. Artemesia vulgaris in Latin), a sacred herb, around our drums to signify that we have the power. We will be unable to get titi paati, so we will have to skip this step. During our return procession, by-standers may ask for healings. We will put a few grains of rice on one side of our drum and beat the underside. The rice will jump and hop. This represents the life energy of the supplicant. If the rice jumps to the south, the direction of death, it will be discarded. If it is jumping unexpectedly high it indicates a desire to leave the earth, and will also be discarded. Sometimes the chaff remaining on the rice separates and even that can mean something. Dark chaff is a bad sign, whereas yellowish chaff is a good sign and indicates prosperity. Aama and Sano Ram will watch the rice to see whether it contains the blessings and the healing needed. When the rice behaves just right it will be dumped over the head of the person asking for healing. Aama will also be offering blessings in the form of tika (red ochre dots on the forehead).

Larry showed us how to handle and use our shaman drums during the shaman dance.

*Learning the Shaman Dance on the roof*
*(Taken by Mujiba Cabugos)*

We rehearsed the Shaman Dance until both Sano Ram and Larry were satisfied with our adeptness. I felt very unprepared and awkward with the dancing and drumming, but I also knew that Spirit would guide me and I would know what I needed when I needed it. I would have liked to have learned the dance earlier in our trip and have practiced it more often.

Next we journeyed into non-ordinary reality to set our intention and call the Spirit guides that will travel with us through the initiation process. Larry drummed while we assumed whatever posture we needed to for the journey. Usually I lay down, but today I sat upright with my face towards the east. Our guides will not be just assisting and bearing witness to the initiation, they will be receiving initiation themselves.

*JOURNEY:*

My Horseshoe Crab led the pack, followed by the Starfish that helps with my extraction work. There were fairies, a white tiger, various Native American spirits who have stood watch as I have increased my knowledge and power. Margaret, Cheilee and Shura are healers I often ask to act as intermediaries between unfamiliar entities and myself. Tattie connects me to Atlantis. The Green Tara shows up but is still in the background. I will learn more about her purpose in my healing as time goes on. Then there is my yi-dam who gave me instructions. The sacred promise I will be making tomorrow will be made three times. This vow is called a Bacha or Bachakl and is a commitment from the heart that can never be broken.

At the end of the non-ordinary reality journey Larry beat his drum in a specific manner, which we refer to as a "callback". I recognized that I would not be coming back fully into ordinary reality, as the initiation had begun for me. In my head background music was continually playing: "Let there be Peace on Earth and let it begin with me."

We were told that, as shamans, we should not eat nettles or pork. Seven Bean Soup was highly recommended but I had already received my own instructions from my yi-dam. I would end my day with plain porridge and hot lemon water. For the next twenty-four hours I would drink only water. My vitamin regimen as well as my blood pressure medication would be unnecessary. Foregoing my daily Toprol tablet required some trust.

After I had eaten, I asked the maitre'd, who was well aware of why we are here, if I could pick a flower from the restaurant garden to take to the shrine tomorrow. He was more than cooperative. He was, in fact, honored that I had asked. I selected three very small but perfect gardenia blossoms that were just coming into fragrant bloom. I probably should have been looking at the marigolds, but the gardenia was the right choice for me.

I laid out my white jeans and white embroidered shirt and chose to wear my old familiar Nikes, because of the support they give me.

I did not sleep well...I was too excited, but in non-ordinary reality there is no sense of time, so the night passed quickly.

# CHAPTER 19
## April 13, 2006 THURSDAY
## FULL MOON SHAMANIC INITIATION

Although the demonstrations continue, some of the shops opened anyway. The city feels like it is returning to normal, but I believe this is only a temporary lull. The curfew has been lifted and mobile phone service has been restored, nevertheless, travel warnings have been heightened and non-essential personal at the US embassy are taking the option of departing Nepal.

Above and beyond all the political unrest, today is what I consider the most important part of this shamanic adventure to Nepal. Today is the Full Moon Shamanic Initiation. It began for me yesterday afternoon and continued with today's pilgrimage.

Our original plan for the Full Moon Initiation was to costume in the early morning and travel by bus to Nagarkot Hill where shamans from all over would be gathering to dance. We would then travel and dance at the Swayambhu Stupa and nearby Balaju Gardens, the Bouddhanath Stupa, and in the evening at the "Place of Dreams". Because of travel restrictions and safety Aama and Larry have restructured the pilgrimage and initiation.

At 5:30 I got up, showered and dressed in the very deliberate manner I have established when I am going to do sacred work. If it were available I would also dunk in salt water, but there is no ocean nearby. I tucked three 1000 rupee notes in my pocket and the three gardenia blossoms. The blooms will be crushed, wilted and brown at the edges by the end of the day, but they are beginning the pilgrimage as exquisitely perfect flowers. Their fragrance lingered on my fingertips.

At 6:00 AM we met on the roof with Aama, Larry, Sano Ram and the rest of the staff who will accompany us on our pilgrimage through the streets to the three shrines Aama and Larry have selected.

We arrived on the roof carrying our brand new shaman drums, and sitting in a single row, facing east, we drummed as the sun rose ever higher through the dusty sky over Kathmandu. Aama went into a trance and took on several personalities as she prepared the way for us. Tiger was very evident as she growled and scratched.

*Erica, Sue and Jeff costuming for the Initiation*
(Taken by Pramod Sapkota)

After this preparation we were dressed in our shaman garb. Aama's helpers costumed us, dropping white gauze skirts over our clothing. Sarah and I had our own white shirts, but the others were given special white shirts with tabs on the shoulders to hold the malas and bell sashes in place. The bell sash is a heavy fabric band that has two-dozen brass bells sewn on it. When Spirit comes into a shaman, the shaman will typically begin to shake -- I do -- thereby ringing the bells and signaling to those present that Spirit has arrived. We have also been wearing the Rittha seed mala that Larry gave each of us when we arrived. It consists of 108 shiny black seeds and is used by shamans for extraction, divination and prayer. The black beads symbolize that the shaman is able to interact with dark spirits. We wear them around our necks, the guru bead at the back, when we are doing Spirit work. When we are not doing Spirit work they are wrapped around the left wrist to indicate that we are shamans and are prepared to offer healings if asked. We were given two Rudraksha seed malas made from wrinkly Elaeocarpus seeds that represent Shiva's tears as he cried with frustration over Brahma's creation and the state of the human condition.  The Rudraksha malas crisscross our chests. With great ceremony a long white cotton headband was stretched out to it's full six-foot length and folded lengthwise to create a four-inch band. It required two people to fold it.  This was then tied securely around our foreheads.  The process was repeated with a red cotton headband, which was secured over the white one. These represent the Rainbow Bridge that connects the secular world with the spirit world. Next came my peacock feather headdress. The feathers are secured in a red and gold brocade band and held upright by porcupine quills.

    I didn't mind the weight of the outfit. I was, as Charles, my brother-in-law would say, "jazzed".  One by one we were costumed and prepared.  June and Burt were last, probably because Burt had had the audacity to ask Aama to dress them first.

    We began to drum as we left the rooftop garden and marched down the stairs, through the lobby and onto the street. Aama, carrying her tiger bone trumpet, led the procession, flanked by Sano Ram and Larry.

*Initiation Procession led by Aama*
*followed by Sano Ram, Larry, Susan and Sarah*
(Taken by Pramod Sapkota)

People came out of shops to watch us pass. Small children fell in stride with us. A woman in a red sari stood in her doorway bowing to us and weeping. At one intersection police were squaring off with a group of protestors and the air was electric with imminent violence. They opened ranks to let us pass and we stopped to do our Shaman Dance and offer blessings. I like to think we diffused the situation, at least temporarily. We marched single file, beating our drums in rhythm with our footsteps.

Initiation Procession filing through the streets as we drummed
(Taken by Pramod Sapkota)

Along the way we stopped and blessed bystanders...and a dog. Every now and then we would pause to do our Shaman Dance.

*The Shaman Dance – Sarah, Susan, Larry, Sano Ram and Aama*
(Taken by Pramod Sapkota)

June began to have problems keeping up. She didn't have the stamina, and the sun was getting higher and hotter. She slung her drum over her shoulder and had all she could do just to walk with us. I found that the hotter and harder it was to walk, the lighter my bell belt felt.

We reached the Indrayani Temple and circumambulated it. This temple honors the eight Mother Goddesses (Ashta Matrika) of the Kathmandu Valley. Our mission was to come for the power of Spirit to take home to our many corners of the world in order to do healings. I was unsure of where to place my offering, as the temple has several structures. I saw a lady drop marigold petals on a carved recess in the pavement that seemed to be a sacred place. There were other flower petals and some fruit on the spot. I dropped one of my gardenias there and realized it was one of the eight Auspicious Signs: The White Lotus, symbolizing purity of body, speech and mind and the blossoming of wholesome deeds in blissful liberation.

*The Lotus auspicious sign with offerings*
(Taken by Pramod Sapkota)

For me it was my first affirmation with my yi-dam. He asked and I responded:

"Do you agree?
Are you capable?
Are you strong enough, powerful enough?
Do you believe?"
"Yes, I agree.
Yes, I am capable.
Yes, I am strong enough, powerful enough.
Yes, I believe."

We crossed the Bishnumati Bridge and proceeded towards a steep stone staircase that led to our next destination.

*Steep Steps to the Temple*
(Taken by Pramod Sapkota)

I heard my logical inner voice say, "You have GOT to be kidding!" when I saw the stone steps, but I was outside the bounds of my normal level of endurance and I squelched the voice and began the long steep climb. The stone steps were old, worn and had varying heights. I had to concentrate on my footing to keep from tripping and I was also dealing with vertigo. At the top of the staircase was our second stop, the Shobha Bhagwati Temple. We entered a courtyard and sat on shaded stone benches to rest. The courtyard was full of small free-standing shrines, very old and intricately carved.

*Courtyard of the Shobha Bhagwati Temple*
*(Taken by Pramod Sapkota)*

    A plodding tortoise about a foot long moved slowly across the courtyard. Doorways opened from all sides of the temple and people filled the openings to watch us. The temple itself is on the far side of the courtyard and Aama prepared to enter on behalf of all of us. A large bell hung in a frame near the entrance to the temple and devotees passed by and rang it at regular intervals. The dog that Larry had blessed and befriended had followed us and, despite all the warnings about touching any dogs, Larry could not resist reaching out to scratch the head of his new canine admirer.

*Dr. Larry's new dog friend. Susan yawning.*
*Yawning is a sign that Spirit is with you.*
*(Taken by Pramod Sapkota)*

People came and went and a crowd gathered to watch us. We were, as you might imagine, quite a sight in our regalia, but even more striking was that we were light-skinned Westerners.

A particular girl in the crowd caught my eye. She had heavier features and darker skin than the average brown-skinned Nepali. She was very thin, very aggressive and had a lost child look about her. I suspect she lives on the streets. I found myself pouring white light towards her, and although she did not look at me directly, she followed our procession for a long distance.

As I sat reflecting, my yi-dam came before me a second time. It was my second affirmation. He asked and I responded:

"Do you agree?
Are you capable?
Are you strong enough, powerful enough?
Do you believe?"
"Yes, I agree.
Yes, I am capable.
Yes, I am strong enough, powerful enough.
Yes, I believe."

After resting, we performed the Shaman Dance for the deities and for the crowd. Aama collected our monetary offerings and entered the temple bringing back red tika with which she blessed each of us individually by rubbing the red dot on our foreheads. I laid my second gardenia, which was becoming quite flattened, on a narrow stone ledge.

Ram is a Brahman and, as such, is qualified to bestow upon us sacred protection threads called "raksha bandhan". He tied them on our wrists - right for men and left for women. As he tied them he was asking for blessings of wisdom and love, and that we be shown our path. The threads represent protection and indicate that we have participated in a sacred ritual. We were instructed to wear the threads until they literally disintegrate. When they fall off we should, according to legend, wait until the Full Moon and then tie them to the tail of a cow in order to ensure that we get into heaven.

We moved down the hill to a third shrine. A little man with a broom was carefully sweeping away flower petals that were littering the area. The statuary image was covered with vermilion ochre, marigold petals and other offerings. It was easy to see where I should leave the third gardenia.

It was here that I made my third and final affirmation. My yi-dam asked and I responded:

"Do you agree?
Are you capable?
Are you strong enough, powerful enough?
Do you believe?"
"Yes, I agree.
Yes, I am capable.
Yes, I am strong enough, powerful enough.
Yes, I believe."

Wrought iron grates that provided roosts for pigeons surrounded the temple. Pigeons in Nepal are just as dirty as they are in the States, so the ground was white with their droppings.

We then descended to the street and passing a Hanuman statue, once again, Erica was ecstatic, bowing and grinning and worshipping her personal hero.

The procession headed back across the bridge, through the dusty streets and toward the hotel. It was mid-day and very hot. Earlier, during the outbound procession, energy had been passed one to the other as we drummed, but there seemed to be a falling off of energy in the middle of the procession where Burt was obviously absorbed in his own discomfort.

*Burt was not having a good time*
*(Taken by Pramod Sapkota)*

It wasn't just that he wasn't transferring energy; he was actually becoming an energy vampire.

I was at the end of the line and Denise was just ahead of me. As Denise became dehydrated I felt the energy that was buoying me up waning, not to mention that I was very concerned about Denise. Pramod ran to get water and Denise revived. Mujiba came around behind us and her strong drumming pulled us back into the fold.

*Mujiba drumming, strong and inspired*
*(Taken by Pramod Sapkota)*

By the time we arrived back at the Tibet Guest House I felt energized, confident and proud to be a shaman. I had accomplished what I had come to Nepal to do.

*Sue Melanson is pleased with the Initiation*
(Taken by Pramod Sapkota)

Larry took me aside and told me how proud he was of the way I handled the initiation. I was strong and consistent and powerful.

My spirit guides had given instructions that I should re-hydrate slowly. First with the hot lemon water and then plain bottled water. If I simply chugged a liter of plain cold water it would over burden my kidneys.

I had given Pramod my camera to record the initiation. When I reviewed the pictures I noticed an abundance of photos of young attractive young women. Pramod had used my camera to flirt. Ah, men!

That evening I had to wait to send my emails because the Internet room was packed. I decided not to go out to dinner with the group, but to eat alone in the hotel dining room and review the day. Over Spaghetti al Fungi (spaghetti with mushrooms) and a Carlsberg beer, I thought about the procession, presenting ourselves at the various temples and the emotional reaction of the people along the way. My pact with my yi-dam was stronger, deeper and more action oriented. Today was the reason I had come to Nepal.

Before falling asleep, which was assisted by the Carlsberg beer, I rubbed Aama's mustard oil on my arthritic knees and the pinched nerve in my back.

Tomorrow is the Nepalese New Year as they enter the year 2063. We aren't meeting until 10 am, so I can celebrate by sleeping in if I so desire.

# CHAPTER 20
## April 14, 2006 FRIDAY
## NEPALI NEW YEAR

A few days ago three new faces appeared in the hotel restaurant. Petite, blond Alison and tall, lanky John are the epitome of the wholesome, All-American couple and they have been waiting for two years to adopt Olivia. Olivia is now 18-months old and they will be able to take her home to Colorado as soon as they receive her immigration visa from the US Embassy. This entire process has been touch-and-go for this young family because adoption regulations in Nepal and immigration regulations in the United States change from time to time. In Nepal the requirements have been known to change with little or no notice. Children under the age of 16 may be adopted as long as they are legally free to be adopted. Under Nepalese law, single mothers, or married mothers who have been left by their husbands, are faced with stringent requirements in order to relinquish their children for adoption. Fathers have twelve years from the child's birth to claim the child and assert custody rights. Unless a mother identifies the father and he agrees in writing to the child's adoption, either willingly or through a court order, the child will not be eligible for adoption. The age difference between prospective parents and the adoptive child must be at least 30 years. The couple must have been married for at least four years prior to filing an application and be declared, by doctor's certification, to be infertile. Single women between the age of 35 and 55 may also adopt. Presently, a family with one child may adopt a child in Nepal of the opposite sex. Two siblings of the opposite sex may be adopted. Families that already have two children may not adopt in Nepal, as the total number of children in a family after the adoption cannot exceed two.

Little Olivia does not seem to be feeling well and is struggling with an upper respiratory ailment. She has been with John and Alison for only a few days and she wants to be held constantly. She seems fussy and they have not seen her smile since they picked her up on Tuesday, but that may be because she has a cold. Alison's sister has supplied them with a wardrobe of hand-me-downs from her fashion-conscious infant twins. Although they are staying in some other hotel, we see them as they come and go to take meals in the Tibet Guest House. Either John or Alison has Olivia in a snuggly close to their hearts. All of us have gotten to know them and we are all concerned about how Olivia is feeling, how Alison and John are holding up, and their progress in getting that all-important visa.

Today is the Nepali New Year and the beginning of their year 2063. We began the day on the roof outside Larry's penthouse. Larry has decided not to pull the plug on this trip just yet. He feels we are safe in the hotel. In honor of the Nepali New Year many shops will be open and we will have some time to shop today, but we are all expected to be vigilant, aware of our surroundings and our personal safety. We should also travel in groups. In line with this, it was brought up that the Australians saw fit to take a taxi to Bouddhanath to visit Aama this morning. Her house is, obviously, a taxi drive away. They went at 6 AM and Burt seemed to get a rush out of brushing up against crowds ready to riot and the accompanying police. Larry told them he is washing his hands of responsibility for their safety since they think they know more than he does. Everyone is concerned with the status of the US Embassy. Larry explained that there is a difference between "giving permission" to the US Embassy personnel to leave the country and "ordered evacuation". So far it is just the former.

We are quite literally living day by day.

King Gyanendra, the 58-year-old monarch, gave his expected speech and vowed to hold elections to "re-energize multi-party democracy". No firm date has been set, but the news broadcasters have suggested it will not be until April 2007. The Seven Party Alliance who are organizing the demonstrations will probably regard this gesture as too little, too late.

Fresh protests erupted this afternoon. Thousands of ordinary people have taken to the streets protesting the actions Gyanendra has taken to eliminate the multi-party system and retain palace control of the country. But the Royal Nepalese Army remains behind the king and that is the key to his power. The United Nations human rights office is taking notice of Nepal's upheaval and issued a statement that their observers are shocked at the excessive force being used by the monarchy against the demonstrators.

Erica, Denise and I were sitting in the lobby towards the end of the day with June and Burt. Erica was snapping pictures of everything from the Durga statue next to the newspaper rack, to the seashell wind chime hanging from the ceiling. She focused on Burt and clicked. She then said, quite jovially, "I hope you don't mind." Burt, however, DID mind. He explained that he didn't like anyone taking his picture and he would tell people as much in no uncertain fashion. Erica was quickly trying to remember how to use the delete function on her camera as Burt continued. During the Initiation Procession we had attracted the attention of several international reporters. We had all been aware of them. Burt, however, not appreciating having his picture taken, described how he had chosen to flip them off. Erica, Denise and I were astonished. If there was ever a picture that would make it to the cover of *Time Magazine*, it would be Burt giving the finger to the reporter and, hence, to the world. We elected Denise to be the one to report the incident to Larry. He should not be taken off guard in case the picture actually did land somewhere important.

We had also observed that both June and Burt have removed their Raksha Bandhan sacred protection threads. It had also occurred to me that it was possible that Aama had instructed Ram not to bestow the threads upon them, thus denying them initiation. The rest of us opted to keep them on, as intended, until they literally fall off.

# CHAPTER 21
## April 15, 2006 SATURDAY
## CONFINED TO THE TIBET GUEST HOUSE

In Nepal the king is regarded as a god. He is, according to tradition, a reincarnation of Vishnu. From the stepped up protests and universal pro-democracy chants, I would ascertain that Gyanendra's sacred status no longer applies. Despite the king's promise to hold elections, the largest protest yet was staged in Kathmandu. The BBC estimates that 8000 participated. There is very little traffic, but some of the shops have opened and we heard that crowds of Nepalis have thronged the vegetable and fruit sellers -- those who have produce to sell. The average citizen is anticipating that the country may be at a standstill for a long time. Seven journalists were wounded today and others have been detained.

Our original itinerary for today would have included a trip to Budhnilkantha where we would have been able to see the gigantic sleeping Vishnu statue that was found buried in the ground in its original state. It is estimated to be 1000 years old. Vishnu is sleeping on a bed of snakes in the middle of a small pond that represents the cosmic water before the universe was created. According to tradition the reigning king of Nepal is not allowed to visit this site. And, because of the reigning king of Nepal, we were not allowed to visit the site either.

Instead we met with Larry on the roof and he told us legends.

In the Golden Age, at the beginning of time, the first shaman lived in a yurt with his nine sisters who were all sorceresses. One of his sisters created a magic mantra and the shaman fell down dead. In the other world he met his guru who told him to go back and make ten rotis (flat breads) for his sisters. He did this. The sisters were ravenous and he threw one roti to each of the sisters. They gobbled up the rotis and then saw the tenth one and they fought for it. One by one they vanquished each other until only the youngest sister was left. Her brother lifted his hand to kill her and she stopped him saying, "Wait! If you kill me, you won't have a job." In other words, "You won't be a shaman." In order to be a shaman you must be able to interact with sorcerers, not kill them.

# CHAPTER 22
## April 16, 2006 SUNDAY
## JEFF'S FEET GO SHOPPING, SANO RAM DOES HEALINGS AND A CHOCOLATE FEAST

I took Jeff's feet shopping with me today. There are only a few shops open, but one of them was Bahini's Boutique just across from the hotel. They carry handmade paper products, Nepali dolls, a wide variety of beads, incense, oils, woodcrafts and jewelry. They also sell Mithila art, which is a contemporary painting style that originates in North India's Bihar state. They feature intricate linear designs based on mythological and folk themes, often depicting the life of deities. These decorative wall pieces are painted with natural plant and mineral-derived colors, using bamboo twigs in lieu of brush or pen. This one depicts Kali.

*"Kali", a Mithila painting*
*(Taken by Sue Melanson)*

In the upstairs over Bahini's is a felt wool studio where they create hand-felted slippers, hats and soft toys. There are simple, no frills slippers in a wide range of color combinations as well as a cuffed variety and silly elf-toe version. Jeff wears size 12 1/2 so I took him with me to buy Art a comfy, cozy pair of felt slippers. After we had selected a deep red pair that fit, I asked the Bahini girls to sew leather soles on so the slippers won't slip. They did it for free. The slippers cost $4.50US. It was such a great deal that I also bought a turquoise and yellow pair for my sister-in-law Terri. We both wear the same size.

Jeff suggested that before we pack all our treasures for the journey home, we should display our purchases and go room to room examining the wares we have all accumulated. The show-and-tell tour never got off the ground, but it was a good idea.

Larry is buying me a duffle bag so I can carry one of his carpets out of the country. I will also be able to pack my extra purchases around it.

Our itinerary for today was supposed to be depossession training with Aama, but she has had to go to southern Nepal where her husband, Buddha, is hospitalized with cancer and, with the continuing strike, she is stranded there.

What to do. What to do. We are all ready to go home.

Sano Ram was able to get to the hotel on foot and he agreed to do healings for us. Ram acts as his interpreter.

I signed up for a Sano Ram healing and was put on the list. The group was invited to follow him from room to room, observing his technique. Each healing I have had since we arrived seems to be like peeling away layers of an onion. Each of these skilled shamans has been able to dig deeper, and Sano Ram dug the deepest yet.

He ascertained that I have a masaan sitting on my vital force. A masaan is a graveyard ghost…a lost spirit that causes spiritual illness and physical problems and is usually controlled by a sorcerer. He says it has been there a long time and the way it "spoils" me relates to my weight, my energy level and stamina, my clarity of thinking, my knees and my arthritis. He also said I have bad dreams that wake me up and I suffer insomnia. I confirmed that I do have insomnia. Sano Ram's recommendation was that I consider having an exorcism ritual (a man chinni) when I return to the States, preferably before my next birthday, which will be May 6 when I turn sixty. Astrologically, the sixtieth year is supposed to be a challenging one with a lot of bad energy associated with it.

I asked Larry whether there was a possibility of doing the depossession ceremony here. Sano Ram and Larry discussed it and agreed to do the ritual at four o'clock tomorrow. It will also be training for my co-adventurers. Larry told the group, including June and Burt, that if anyone is planning to attend with negative energy they will be asked to leave. I feel I am in good hands, and have great hope for this ritual. It is the beginning of the rest of my life.

Under normal circumstances I would provide the materials Sano Ram needs for the ritual and my whole family would be involved in the process. But we can't go out, so Sano Ram has agreed to bring whatever is necessary and I will pay him. I am preparing, as I did for the initiation. I will eat only porridge and lemon water for supper. Susan takes great notes, almost verbatim, and I have asked her to take notes for me. Mujiba's notes are much more esoteric, but her notes will be helpful, too. Denise says this is a great relief for everyone -- we are actually going to do something positive. This is, apparently, my second reason for coming Nepal. Aama will try to get here tomorrow, but I doubt she will make it.

It's been a good day. I am grateful for the rooftop garden where the whole world seems normal - or normal for Kathmandu. It is very frustrating watching the political situation from within the hotel walls. All we can do is send small ripples of healing into a very troubled universe.

I am very honored to have been the "patient" today. Tomorrow is the depossession ceremony. Tuesday morning we will process what happens tomorrow, finishing packing, and begin the journey home. That may involve a whole new set of adventures, but the end will justify whatever we encounter.

In celebration mode, Denise and I went to the corner shop and bought HUGE bars of Belgium chocolate. We brought them back and devoured all 200 grams of milk chocolate in the restaurant garden accompanied by tea…and we called it dinner.

# CHAPTER 23
## April 17, 2006 MONDAY
## THE MAN CHINNI DEPOSSESSION CEREMONY

My gastro-intestinal tract was bemoaning the chocolate feast Denise and I had indulged in for dinner. No one should ever eat 200 grams of chocolate at one sitting.

The anti-royalist protests continue and this is the twelfth day of the strike. Garbage is piling up in the streets and wandering cows and dogs prowl the neighborhood heaps. There is both a fuel and food shortage, and prices are beginning to rise sharply as the entire country experiences panic buying. No one knows how long this will last.

We met with Larry on the roof to go over what a "man chinni" (depossession ceremony) entails. He explained that the ceremony is a barter ritual in which the shaman will entice the masaan to leave the afflicted patient. The ritual involves four steps: 1.) Identifying the source of the problem. 2.) Severing the hold the possessing entity has on the patient. 3.) Tranferring of the possessing entity into a surrogate effigy. 4) Moving the afflicting entity on to their proper place.

A shaman spends time establishing a relationship with spirits, both good and evil. He/she earns a reputation for honoring both light and dark, having enlightenment and compassion for the entire universe. Not just the good parts. In a possession situation, the resulting illness is considered a consumptive process, as the hungry masaan devours the parts if its host that it craves, be it energy, power, or life-force. It needs to be re-directed to a place where it is harmless. In order to do this the shaman will lure the masaan from its host by offering a feast to be held in its honor. Some masaans are drawn to individual foods, while others crave energy, or simply attention, and some just want the opportunity to bask in the limelight.

In the Golden Age, at the beginning of time, the power of the sun was decreasing. The gods needed fire to renew it and humans had fire. The gods chose a chicken as a messenger to go and ask the humans for some of their fire. But the chicken was constrained by one condition the gods made. He could not crow for the humans. He was allowed to make the deal for the fire, but he could not crow, if he did he would die. When the chicken came to the humans they told him that they would only give him fire if he crowed for them. The chicken became tired of arguing and decided it was better to break the interdiction and crow, rather than risk not getting the fire. So he crowed. Thus the chicken was selected to be willing to give his life in order to save a human life. A chicken that is thus dispatched finds immortality. But it has to agree willingly. During a depossession ceremony, if a chicken sacrifice is necessary, the chicken will be asked if it is willing. There are various ways in which the chicken will signify that it is willing.

The shaman will then sacrifice the chicken and the dead animal will be cooked for a feast of all present except the shaman and the patient who are forbidden to eat of the sacrifice.

Since we intended to use my hotel room for the depossession ceremony we will, obviously, be unable to perform a chicken sacrifice. (If we had a chicken to sacrifice!)

In a traditional depossession ceremony the entire family of the patient helps with preparations. They create an effigy from clay, then they carve details into it with a pin making as many details and body parts as can be depicted. They dress it, hoping the masaan will like the effigy better than the patient's body. Obviously most masaans are not intellectually astute. Then they collect and bring all sorts of offerings to the masaan. Since we could not get out to collect the various offerings Sano Ram brought what was needed.

I had seen a depossession ceremony before and knew that a Prasad or Holy Meal followed the ceremony and I was willing to have the kitchen help me create a platter of fruit for that purpose, but Larry assured me Sano Ram had it all under control. I suppose I was not being sensitive to the restrictions the kitchen was under either. They would have been hard pressed to fill my request because of the strike and curfew and the increasingly serious food shortage.

I tidied up my room and moved my suitcases into the bathtub so there would be room for everyone. I slid the little table I used for my altar between the beds. Sano Ram knocked at my hotel room door with Larry, Ram and Pramod. They had a whole array of bags and packages with them. Members of our group arrived to witness the ceremony and take notes. To my surprise, June and Burt came. Burt did not readily find a place to sit so he cleared my altar in one swoop and sat down on it. I would have objected but it happened so fast that I barely had time to notice.

*Materials used to create the man chinni*
*(Taken by Pramod Sapkota)*

Sano Ram laid a tablecloth from the dining room on the floor to protect the rug. He then began to create an effigy, or Lui, on the floor by sifting cornmeal between his fingers. The image he created was about 2 feet tall and I watched in fascination as he kept adding details to it...a moustache, ribs, fingers and toes, and, eventually, a substantial penis. This was a MALE Lui...no doubt.

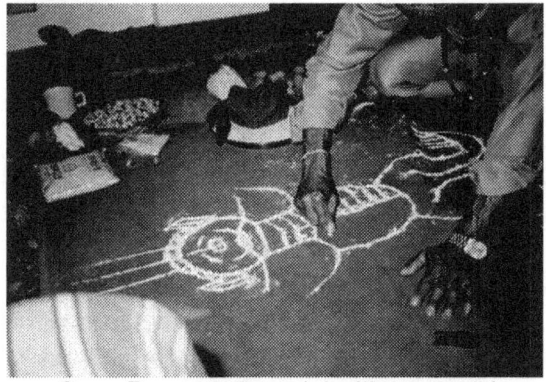

*Sano Ram creates a lui with cornmeal*
*(Taken by Mujiba Cabugos)*

Sano Ram then began to arrange offerings to entice the masaan. The object of this ritual was to make the Lui attractive and honoring to the masaan. He made a pile of rice over the Lui's heart and nestled one perfect hen egg on it. This would be the substitute for the live chicken. He created nine oil pots by filling shallow terra cotta bowls with mustard oil and putting wicks in them. These he placed on each hand, on each foot, on the Lui's root charka, on his heart and three above his head. Sano Ram then filled nine terra cotta water pots with alcohol and water and put a few grains of rice, and bits of red, white or yellow flowers in each of them. These also went on each hand, each foot, three at the top of his head, one on the heart and one on the groin. Next he then placed a Betel Nut above the egg. Betel nuts are chewed and can be made into Pan Massala, which is a narcotic concoction. A very enticing vice for a hungry masaan! Red tika was then put on the egg, honoring it. He then took a large square of red fabric and tore it into five pieces. These he put at the four corners of the Lui and the fifth near its heart. He did the same with a green piece of fabric making four more "flags" and placed them next to the red squares. Ram explained that ordinarily they would use a variety of colors, but this time they could only find red and green. These flags represented the nine planets. On each flag Sano Ram laid out offerings for the masaan's feast. On each fabric square he placed a piece of banana, a slice of apple, sections of orange, candy and chocolate (an offering Sano Ram rarely brings), rice, beans, corn, grains, cornmeal, three braids of incense and a few coins. Sano Ram then took three large Sal tree leaves. On the first he put rice and red tika representing Hanuman. On the second he put rice and yellow tika representing Vishnu. On the third he put rice and holy ash from the hardwood tree, Shorea Robusta, representing Shiva. These three leaves he placed in front of him. He had created a bowl-like basket from Sal tree leaves and into this basket he put flowers and sprinkled water over them. The object of the ritual was to lure the masaan into this basket. Each of the red and green flags looked like mini-altars. Next he scattered rice then dried corn over the Lui. This was indeed a very detailed, very enticing Lui and the masaan was watching carefully.

Next Sano Ram passed a cup around the room and asked each of those present to add pieces of themselves. He requested a strand of hair, a toenail clipping, a fingernail clipping and a string from their clothing. He began by collecting these offerings from me and handed the cup around. Everyone in the room got busy clipping and snipping, except June and Burt. They were not very participatory. When the collection was complete, Sano Ram sprinkled the clippings and snippings on the Lui's forehead.

*The lui surrounded by lavish offerings*
*(Taken by Pramod Sapkota)*

Sano Ram then tied five-colored rainbow strings around my head and shoulders and extended them across the Lui to the Sal leaf basket. If there had been a clay Lui used in the ritual, the strings would have extended from my head and shoulders and have been tied around the Lui's neck. The white string connects the bones of the patient to the lui, the red string connects the patient's blood, the yellow connects the flesh, the green string connects the hair, and the blue string connects the breath of the patient.

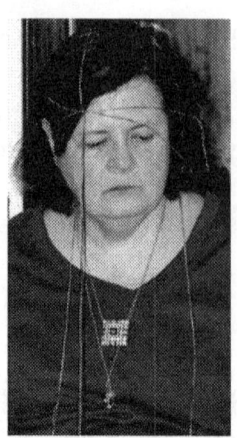

*Sano Ram tied rainbow string around
the patients' head and shoulders*
(Taken by Pramod Sapkota)

Sano Ram then lit nine incense braids and nine incense sticks in a metal burner, as he called upon his guru and the deities, especially Kali, to assist. He would also have lit the nine oil lamps but it was too risky in a crowded hotel room. One has to do what makes sense! He then stood in front of me and gave the masaan notice that the ceremony was about to begin. I was fully aware of everything, but I also sensed that my own identity was taking a backseat to the entity Sano Ram was addressing. He began his mantra, placing a handful of rice over my head throwing it in the Sal leaf basket. He then held rice near my heart and threw that into the Lui. He repeated this three times.

*Sano Ram addresses the offending masaan*
(Taken by Pramod Sapkota)

Sano Ram then addressed the masaan and listed all the offerings that were being served up as a sacred meal just for it. Burning incense filled the air. As Sano Ram tried to entice the masaan I felt an almost physical movement within me. It was a sensation similar to feeling my baby kick for the first time when I was pregnant. The masaan had liked the sound of a male body and the power it offered. It also liked CHOCOLATE. Perhaps the meal Denise and I had enjoyed the evening before was directed by the masaan in an attempt to get one last fix before being forced to move out of my body.

Sano Ram sat on the floor next to the incense and began to chant his mantra, rocking slightly. This went on for what seemed like a long time.

I shut my eyes and felt myself begin to shake. This masaan had been with me a long time and it was unwilling to leave. The masaan then attempted to call upon the sorceress that controlled it. A woman's name came to me but it meant nothing. Then I suddenly saw an image...a flashback to 1994 when I was managing a mall in Salem, Massachusetts. One of my security guards was Wiccan and part of a coven. Alex had preached his Wiccan beliefs to me for awhile until he gathered that I was uninterested. But, Salem being Salem, I did appreciate his perspective and sometimes asked his opinion on things touching on witchcraft such as, was that dead black cat on the loading dock a deliberate sign or was it just a cat who had eaten a De-Con infested rat. Alex also had a girlfriend and they were both part of the same coven. One day she came to pick Alex up for lunch. She was dressed in a red spandex dress that barely covered her crotch and stopped just above her nipples. She wore spike heel black leather boots that came over her knees. Around her forehead was a black velvet band with a red jewel hanging at the middle of her forehead. Instead of a necklace she wore a spiked dog collar. I asked Alex if she always dressed that way and he snickered and responded, "No, only when she wants to play." What I did not know at the time was that she was not there for Alex that day...she was there for me. Perhaps she sensed the power I was coming into. Perhaps I threatened her in some way. In any case, this poor starving masaan...probably some wandering spirit rescued from a Salem graveyard...was under her control and had been sitting on my vital force for twelve years. The effect of its presence showed up in my metabolism, my weight, my stamina and my energy level. This possession was not a random event. It was clearly intentional and premeditated and controlled by a very powerful sorceress.

Sano Ram threatened, bartered and negotiated trying to get the masaan to follow the colored string to the Sal leaf bowl. At one point the masaan tried to call out to his sorceress. I could feel myself becoming more and more detached from my body. Suddenly my eyes opened, involuntarily, and I looked hard at Sano Ram. Pramod snapped a photograph at this exact moment and caught the look. The eyes looking at Sano Ram were not mine.

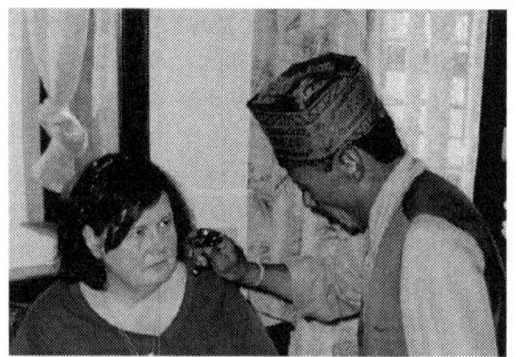

*The eyes of the masaan*
*(Taken by Pramod Sapkota)*

Sano Ram saw the shift and guided the masaan along the colored strings, across the Lui and into the Sal leaf bowl. He returned to check to be certain it was not hiding in my heart...a place masaans like to hide, but the masaan was gone. It had moved to the offering bowl. Sano Ram quickly cut the rainbow strings, guaranteeing that the masaan could not retrace its steps and re-enter my body and Mujiba stood me up and turned me around. The pieces of cut string went into the Sal leaf basket with the masaan. He held the three leaves of ochre and ash over my head and chanted "Om Om Om" followed by "Phoot Phoot Phoot" which means "Go Go Go". There was a scurry of activity as all the offerings were piled into the Sal leaf bowl and a lid placed on it. Sano Ram used the heel of his hand on the Lui to keep it down. He then folded up the tablecloth under the Lui, containing everything on the cloth and placed that in the Sal leaf basket. He then blew blessings on my head, heart and shoulders. To be certain the connection with the masaan was severed Sano Ram cut the space over my head and around my shoulders with first the iron knife, then with the phurba and finally he used his mala to bless me and ensure the masaan was gone. The Sal leaf basket was then carried from the room as Sano Ram shouted "Phoot Phoot Phoot" (Go Go Go) over and over. Ram was interpreting and told everyone that Sano Ram would throw it in the river as he went home that evening. That's where "spoiling" spirits are sent to be neutralized. Sano Ram then returned to the room, put holy ash on my forehead, shoulders, hands and knees.

The ritual part of the ceremony was over. A lighter atmosphere filled the room and Sano Ram peeled apples and bananas and shared them with everyone. This was the symbolic holy meal called a Prasad.

I asked what Sano Ram had seen. Through Ram he replied, "After this process, your body will be free from the masaan. My [Sano Ram's] spirit deity has taken out the masaan. You are free from it. And everyone in the room got healed as a result. There will be peace in you and in all of us."

If we had had the opportunity, we would have gone as a group to find a sacred tree bringing with us rice and tika offerings. Once there we would have circled the tree with white thread, once for every year of our age. This ritual would lift Bad Days and Planets from me as well as everyone in the group. And considering the number of us entering our $60^{th}$ year, that was important.

The group began to depart and Sano Ram cleaned up the ceremonial area. I asked whether the sorceress that had controlled the masaan was aware of this ceremony. Sano Ram looked stern and told me that she was very aware. He asked whether I knew where the masaan came from. I told him I was pretty sure I did. He asked whether I have occasion to go to the place where the sorceress is. I told him I did not. He advised me to stay away from that place. That place is Salem, Massachusetts.

I reconstructed my altar on my desk, figuring that Burt's butt had desecrated the little table. Then I lay down, exhausted, excited and very thirsty. I didn't feel quite present.

We settled up our accounts with the hotel front desk. All our breakfasts have been included, but we pay for lunches, most dinners, bottled water and Internet time. I have been signing most of these expenses to my room and I was expecting a sizeable bill for the fifteen days we have been here (pre-Pokhara and post-Pokhara). The grand total was 4760 rupees, which translates to less than $75 US.

We are allowed two carry-on pieces of luggage, which includes a pocketbook. I have a courier style daypack into which my purse will fit. My second carry-on will be my shaman drum. Most of us are carrying our drums. I am checking Larry's duffle bag through to LAX with one of his carpets and some of my stuff. My big suitcase is chock-a-block full. I am leaving behind a lot of toiletry items. My apothecary items have been added to Larry's collection that he will leave in Nepal for use by future groups including Imodium, various Chinese herbs and some of my own herbal remedies.

Sano Ram came with his grandson today and our fellow adventurers gave the little boy all sorts of gifts such as a baseball cap, a child's board game and little toys. I hadn't brought any child-appropriate gifts.

I had brought bottles of our own maple syrup and pancake mix for Larry's staff. Everyone seemed very appreciative except Gauri who refused to allow me to give him anything. He actually jumped over the lobby coffee table to put furniture between us almost as if I was attacking him.

I gave my "Fodor's Guide to Nepal, Bhutan and Tibet" to Pramod and, at Larry's suggestion, Michael Harner's "Way of the Shaman" to Jigme.

I gave the maitre'd, who has been more than accommodating, a gift of Maine maple syrup and packs of cigarettes for his staff. Every little gesture today seems like a ceremonial separation from a life we have known briefly and will never know again. As anxious as I am to be on my way home, it is sad to be making these closures.

I had one more closure to make. I owed Shaym, the tee shirt man, a few rupees for the extra embroidery he did on my white shirt and I didn't want to forget. I darted across the alley to pay the balance. It was minimal to me but makes a lot of difference to him. Shaym had been asking everyone heading for the States if they lived near New Hampshire. Months ago a tourist had ordered a tee shirt and never picked it up. I volunteered to take it home and mail it to the fellow. It was an orange tee shirt with a silver-winged dragonfly on it embroidered "Dragonfly Heaven". It was very special to someone. Shaym's wife bowed and thanked me profusely and gave me a cute little silk change purse as a gift.

In preparation for going through customs we have collected receipts for our purchases. Any archeological objects, or objects that look like they may be very old, require a special stamp, as do bone objects and Thangkas.

Our itinerary called for a late night going away party. Because of the food shortage Larry felt it would be inappropriate to throw a gastronomical fling, but we did gather for a final meal with all the staff. We haven't seen Suju in over a week. Without being able to use the bus we have had no need for a driver. It was good to see him. Jigme, Suju and Pramod got into a political debate and Pramod began to express his anti-monarchy views with great emotion. Larry leaned over to a couple of us and whispered, "I worry about his future in this country."

Until tonight I think the gravity of our situation in Nepal has been something I have chosen to ignore. The political unrest does not look like it is going to let up any time soon. The Maoists are active and it is time to go home.

# CHAPTER 24
## April 18, 2006 TUESDAY
## DEPARTING KATHMANDU

Every evening since I had moved to Room 207, my days have ended with the annoying beat of June and Burt drumming. And every evening the drumming has become more erratic and cacophonous. This evening, their percussion became unbearable even to Mother Nature. Our last night in Kathmandu was interrupted by tumultuous weather. During the night tremendous thunderstorms came through the valley and buffeted the hotel. Booming thunder and lightening accompanied the high winds, as if Mother Nature were reacting to both the Australian drumming and the upheaval in the streets. At one point there was a terrific crack and the power went out. I was afraid Larry's penthouse had been hit. I considered shutting my windows but opted to pull the covers over my head like a little girl and just wait it out. The storm continued, but at least the drumming stopped.

This morning's local news continues to be grim. Oil tanker trucks of fuel from India are unable to reach major cities and a fuel shortage has gripped Kathmandu. Many gas stations have shut down, supposedly, to check rampant black marketing. All private airlines will cease domestic operations today. The hotel has been forced to add a 25% food surcharge because of the food shortage.

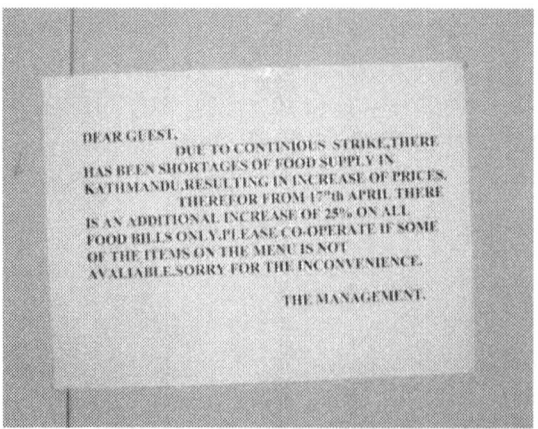

And the areas largest wholesale vegetable market is closing April 20th.

Baby Olivia and her new parents are still waiting for the visa that will allow them to go home to Colorado.

I was disappointed that the plan to process yesterday's Depossession Ceremony dropped through the cracks, as I never had a chance to hear what others thought about the experience or to fill them in on my own insights. Everyone is focused on packing and heading for home.

Larry has decided to leave with us. He had planned to stay for a while, but he has been able to get a plane ticket to Delhi and he will make arrangements to get to Los Angeles from there. It is definitely time to "Get Outta Dodge!"

Larry was behind closed doors with the owner of the Tibet Guest House squaring up the account for all of us. The owner then appeared to wish us a safe journey and gave each of us a tee shirt advertising the hotel.

We thought we had said all our good byes when through the lobby door walked Aama. She was all smiles and blessed each of us with a gold katag and a packet of braided incense. All of us became weepy as we hugged our grandmother shaman.

To expedite the airport process, we all gave Sarah money for the exit taxes and porter's tip. At 9:30 AM sharp we crammed into the hotel vans and headed for the airport. It was quite a seating arrangement since we were all carrying our shaman drums. Those phurba handles were awkward.

On the way to the airport the vans stopped for gas. Larry was annoyed at the delay since the gas gauge read half full, but the driver explained that unless he had tourists in the car a TOURIST ONLY vehicle would not get gas. At first it seemed like we were in line forever and then we were shuffled around and suddenly the gas was being pumped.

We were stopped at the entrance to the airport and the van driver assured the guards that we had plane reservations. At the terminal there were long lines of departing people. We grabbed a cart and a porter and began to wait. The line moved quickly...so quickly that Larry's luggage got ahead of us and was heading for the wrong plane. After we passed the first security x-ray and frisk, the porters helped herd us to the check-in desk. Sarah was busy arranging seating on the plane and lost track of the porters waiting for their tip. When she did break away to pay them she turned towards them with a wad of loose rupee notes as if she was offering them the entire handful. As it turned out most of us tipped the porters ourselves just to get through the confusion. Sarah then took our money to the bank across the lobby to buy exit tax tickets. She collected our airline tickets and passports and we received our Thai Air boarding passes that would get us to Bangkok. Our bags were checked direct to LAX.

We then took an escalator upstairs, through passport control, and turned in our departure cards.

There was a brief lull in the bustle of activity and we plopped down in a waiting area surrounded by concession stands, shops and last minute places to drop a rupee or two. I had been looking for a key chain for my friend Barbara. Her husband has Multiple Sclerosis and has been in a veterans' facility for years. She keeps him in touch with the world by constantly adding to his key chain collection. I had promised her something really neat from Nepal. I found the key chain I was looking for in one of those shops. I had also been craving a croissant and I found one. There were lots of postcards and that copulating elephant card was available on a computer mouse pad. I was only vaguely aware that I had no interest in the Snickers, Milky Way or M&Ms that were prominently displayed.

There was yet another security checkpoint, and although we were frisked and our carry-ons searched, the fact that we were carrying shaman drums seemed to mean something. The little man who searched my daypack asked what the mustard oil from Aama was. He then picked up my drum and placed it reverently on the table, bowed to me and said "Namaste".

We passed one final checkpoint and found ourselves in a huge, crowded waiting room overlooking the tarmac. Larry had been negotiating a different set of check-ins but he, too, ended up in the same waiting room. Everyone was leaving Kathmandu. Now we just had to wait. Our flight was scheduled to depart at 2:40 PM and we were required to be there two hours ahead of time. I dozed in the waiting room chairs partly because I was exhausted and partly because I didn't want to think about the three-day flight ahead.

Finally the BOARDING sign flashed, everyone hugged Larry and we headed out across the tarmac on foot to climb the steps onto the plane.

We were finally going home!

## CHAPTER 25
## April 18, 19 and 20, 2006
## THREE DAYS TRAVEL, WEST TO EAST

My seatmate on Thai Air was a young lady from Kathmandu who was traveling with her boss to Louisville, Kentucky where they were going to be doing a trade show in an attempt to find wholesale buyers for Nepali bronze pieces. Her enthusiasm was shielded by cultural constraints of decorum, but I got her talking about the bronzes that were traveling with them in the underbelly of the plane, the possibilities the trade show might afford and what the entire venture might mean to her company, her family and to her personally. She was radiant with expectation.

We arrived in Bangkok in daylight. The air was hot, humid and heavy. On the horizon we could see the skyscrapers of the city but we didn't have enough time to tour around.

Larry had raved about the massage services at the airport and that sounded good to everyone. I, on the other hand, have massages regularly, and I know how much water I have to drink to remove the wastes stirred up by a good massage. It didn't seem prudent to me to have a massage before an intercontinental flight. I was also very tired.

Denise and I shared a room in the Amari Airport Hotel again and this time housekeeping arrived to separate the twin beds that lay beneath the king size bedspread. The group was heading for dinner but I was more tired than hungry. It never occurred to me that I would be unable to catch up with them if I changed my mind. I am so used to having cell phone connections in the States – even in a big store I can locate Art two aisles away. So I slept!

Eventually I did wake up, and discovered that the air conditioning was not keeping up with the heat and that I had become hungry. I looked at the room service menu, considered wandering around, and then explored the mini-bar in the room. Not only was there wine and beer, but sodas, bottled water and snacks. My dinner that evening was a wine spritzer and a can of Pringles potato chips. The cost for this indulgence was $8 US.

Denise came "home" and we slept fitfully in the A/C challenged room.

The next morning everyone headed for more massages and breakfast in the airport. This time I was determined to take Carol Peters' advice and have breakfast at the Zeppelin Restaurant. The buffet was set up in an oval that must have been thirty feet long with every possible breakfast food, pastry and fruit juice imaginable...Tibetan, American, European, Indian, Chinese...it was all there. I chose an omelet made with goat cheese and "fungi" (mushrooms), some spicy home-fried potatoes, a croissant, a berry medley with whipped cream and fresh squeezed orange juice. A waitress appeared to fill my coffee cup with a heavenly blend of good strong French Roast coffee and offered me a newspaper. The Nepali news was three sentences on page 18. The demonstrations were continuing. The front page was full of Thailand's news. They were experiencing their own brand of unrest.

After breakfast I sent an email to Art from the Business Center telling him I had reached Bangkok. I knew he would be relieved to know that we had successfully departed Kathmandu.

My next quest was to get a manicure and pedicure. I may be a farm girl from Maine, but there are some luxuries I missed during my three weeks in Nepal. I was the first customer at the lobby beauty salon and I had to communicate with the nail tech through a youthful hair stylist. Youth had on a brown tank top with cursive letters across the boobs that read "I Can Fly". On the back were sewn tiny pink wings. I emerged with my toes shiny and red and my fingertips groomed. I considered having a haircut, but I knew I would be at risk if Youth didn't understand my instructions.

In my sandals, with my bare toes still drying, I sat in the Amari lobby people-watching and enjoying a Cappuccino. Eventually Denise appeared and sat with me. We ordered dainty tea sandwiches and cookies as we sat beside the lobby waterfall where live water lilies floated in full bloom.

As our flight departure time to Taipei drew near everyone appeared with his or her luggage and shaman drums in hand.

Between Bangkok and Taipei I sat with an aggressively chatty oriental woman who was building a house in Thailand. At first I thought she meant she was cutting the lumber, hauling the stucco and pounding the nails, but I soon ascertained that she was the architect.

On the ground in Taipei we had lunch in an airport restaurant and discovered a Baskin & Robbins ice cream stand. Mujiba ordered a double chocolate ice cream cone. In the past I would have done the same, BUT the masaan's craving for chocolate no longer controlled me. The reality of the healing was startling. I had been cured of chocolate! So I ordered a lemon sherbet.

In Taipei Jeff looked into upgrading to Business Class for the long flight to California. Unfortunately the code on our tickets did not allow him to do that and all the Business Class seats had already been spoken for. Sarah arrived with our boarding passes and we discovered that we were all spread throughout the massive coach cabin. Jeff and I somehow ended up side-by-side two aisles from the very back of the plane. Erica was behind us against the back bulkhead.

The flight was rough and those of us in the back felt it the most. Across the aisle a fashionable young lady in a sari had to use the barf bag as her attentive young husband rubbed the back of her neck. Throwing up has a contagious affect...like yawning. Once someone does it, others follow suit, so I sucked on a Ginger Chew and listened to classical music on the headphones. I wanted to maintain the same regimen Denise and I had established coming over by getting up to walk and stretch, but the lady on the other side of me had taken a sleeping pill and was out cold. I managed to crawl over her a couple of times to use the ladies room, but for the most part I just stayed put. The noisy turbulence made it too hard to carry on conversation, so I wasn't able to chat with Jeff. But there were benefits of sitting together. We lifted the armrest between us to allow a teeny bit more space; Jeff was more than happy to take my extra dessert; and I wasn't as embarrassed as I might have been when I woke up drooling on Jeff's shoulder. We watched movies and slept. The trip was uneventful, except for the meals. And, as I never barfed and we didn't crash, I considered the trip a success.

I was becoming increasingly aware of how much I missed the United States. I couldn't wait to set foot on US soil. I played the "Star Spangled Banner" in my head, and the stirring Lee Greenwood song "God Bless the USA."

> *"And I'm proud to be an American*
> *where at least I know I'm free.*
> *And I won't forget the men who died,*
> *who gave that right to me.*
> *And I'd gladly stand up next to you*
> *and defend her still today.*
> *'Cause there ain't no doubt I love this land*
> *God bless the U.S.A."*

My heart and my eyes were overflowing with emotion, but I was really really quiet about it. I was on my way home and that was the bottom line. No one else needed to see or share my personal anticipation. And Jeff was asleep.

Once on the ground at LAX we gathered at the baggage carousel waiting for our luggage that had been checked straight through from Kathmandu. Jeff's floral luggage was always readily identifiable and we all had learned to look for ours close behind. It suddenly occurred to me that it was almost over. As soon as our bags showed up and we maneuvered customs, we'd be hustling off in different directions. Most of the group had connecting flights to catch. Denise had a hotel room as she waited for her early morning flight to Oregon. Sarah and I were going to meet Larry's son, Aaron. This was the end of our temporary family…the Mother Hen and her peeps. As the arrival of each piece of luggage signaled the release of each adventurer to individual journeys, there were hugs and hasty good-byes. None of us would grasp the finality of it for days.

Aaron found Sarah and I and bundled us into the Peters SUV. We dropped Sarah at Southwest Air and then on to Topanga Canyon where I was to spend the night. I helped swing the dragon gate open and the dogs greeted us. Carol Peters was with "Heart" taping a VH1 concert. Aaron let me into the house, and headed home to his pregnant wife, and then I was alone. I knew which room was mine. I knew where the light switch was. I knew that Belle would stay with me until she heard Carol come home. It was comfortingly familiar…and I was on US soil…at last.

I called Art to confirm "The Eagle Has Landed". One more day and I would be sleeping in my own bed, but for one more night I appreciated being able to sleep in Jemma's bed. At the foot of her bed is her dragon carpet.

The next day I had time to visit briefly with Carol and gave her a quick overview of the trip. I expressed my bewilderment at how the Australians had come to be part of our group. Carol looked surprised. She said "Didn't you know that Sarah sponsored them?" Quite frankly, I didn't know Sarah had any connection with them whatsoever.

Carol had to rush off to a dental appointment and Aaron came to take me to the airport. Larry's family was so very generous with their time and hospitality.

I checked in at Delta and found that my big suitcase was overweight. I had to pay a surcharge of $25 but I didn't care! Just get me and my luggage home!

There was the usual x-ray machine and metal detector. Everyone had to send his or her shoes through the x-ray machine. But the days of being frisked and going through customs were over.

The first leg of the cross-country flight took me from Los Angeles to Cincinnati. I sat with an interesting young artist who lived in the Netherlands near the Belgium border. He was an American who had chosen to live abroad and he had been visiting his family in California. His claim to fame were grandiose collages that he created from pictures of body parts clipped from "Playboy" Magazines. I asked whether there was a copyright infringement in that kind of work. He responded that he sincerely hoped so. It would bring wonderful publicity. I asked who typically buys his artwork. He laughed and said "Art collectors with too much money and too much wall space." He was on his way back to Europe to prepare for a showing in Rotterdam.

My layover in Ohio seemed endless. I was anxious to complete the last part of my journey. I ate a wilted salad in McDonald's while I waited and read a hand-me-down newspaper.

I felt sticky and tired, so I washed my face and neck in the ladies room being very careful not to chip my new nail polish. I gave my hair a good brushing for no other reason than to kill time. Finally, we boarded!

Art and I have always been able to "feel" one another. I know when his car is coming up the mountain late at night. He knows when I cross the border into Maine after a weekend in Massachusetts. I knew he could feel my plane winging closer. I knew he would be waiting.

Just before 11 PM EST, the night sky opened over Portland. I could see the lights of the Maine Mall and the reflections off the water that weaves its way up to Stroudwater. Rows of lights told me where the major highways were and then...we were on the ground. And minutes later I was in Art's arms crying. I was home!

# CHAPTER 26
# BACK IN MY REAL WORLD

The first things I noticed were the smells. As Art enveloped me in a bear hug I could smell his Kanon aftershave, and the distinctly Art smell of his hair, his skin and the worn wool jacket he was wearing. As we walked to the car I could smell the Maine air. Although the night was overcast, the air was crisp and clean and I could smell the ocean. The leather seats in the car had a whiff of lemon that indicated Art had taken the Caddy through the car wash recently. I sank into the familiar comfort of the passenger seat, which was not too hard, not to soft…it was just right!

I talked non-stop from the airport to South Hiram. As we turned to climb Tripptown Road up the mountain to home, I looked over at Stanley Pond. Spring peepers were serenading. The pond had been frozen when I left. The woods had leafed out and the birds had arrived for the summer. I had missed an entire month of spring unfolding in the magical foothills of southwestern Maine.

We turned into the long driveway to Oak Hill Farm, aptly called Husky Haven, and passed the dog pens where our Siberian Huskies, Princess and Ted, poked their heads out of their doghouses to see whether someone was inadvertently going to feed them at 1 AM.

We decided to unload the car the next day, so I just brought in what I was carrying.

Inside, the house was immaculate. Art had single-handedly assembled the summer breakfast porch (which held our firewood in the winter), cleaned the house, top to bottom, and he had even smudged each room. He must have missed me very much, or been very bored while I was gone. In addition to the house, he had managed to mothball the maple syrup operation, pulling every one of our 1000 taps and washing the two plus miles of tubing by himself. When I had left, the sap was still flowing.

I had missed the sentient feel of Oak Hill. I had been to the Himalayas, but these were the rocks and hills, trees and streams that resonated with me. This feeling was why we decided to settle here.

My first focus was a luxurious shower, during which I allowed water to fill my mouth as I gargled the pure mountain spring water with no fear of what lurked in each droplet. My bed awaited me with freshly laundered sheets and my own perfect pillow...not too hard, not too soft...just right! I could see the stars out the window above my head in the crystal clear night sky and everything was still, silent and sleeping. There was no hum of the city, no barking dogs, no didgeridoo playing in the courtyard, no June and Burt drumming and no need for white noise to fall asleep.

Breakfast began with coffee, made in a coffee maker controlled by a timer so it was there when we woke up. Cheerios with banana never tasted so good!

Common sense dictated that I run through a full course of Cipro once I got home. It took a couple of weeks for my system to adjust. And there was jet lag, which presented itself as aching muscles, erratic sleep patterns and an overall unbalanced feeling. Fortunately Art had our masseuse booked the day after I got home to speed the integration process.

I used up Aama's mustard oil on my knees and lower back and they are amazingly improved. (Art was not impressed that our bed sheets smelled like stir-fry every evening.)

I added a Durga and my little "jade" Ganesh to my altar. The dragon carpet is on the floor at the foot of our bed.

But the most dramatic change was my release from the masaan that had been "spoiling" me. Chocolate does not interest me in the least. A Preston Jones Pig Out Chocolate Chip Cookie could not tempt me. I dropped twelve pounds quickly and after that a slower gradual weight loss began. My stamina, energy level and clarity of thought are all significantly improved.

Since we had never found a tree in Nepal to wrap string around for every year of my life, I climbed halfway up Oak Hill to Grandfather Oak. I asked permission and then decorated his venerable trunk with sixty turns of string.

The Raksha Bandhan sacred protection strings that were tied on my left wrist during the initiation became more and more threadbare as time went on. As they tattered I used hair gel to try to re-weave them, but eventually they did fall off after over three months. I haven't found a cow with a tail to tie them to yet.

I mailed the "Dragonfly Heaven" tee shirt off to its Merrimack, NH owner. The recipient had thought his special order would never make it to the US. He had had it made for his friend, Helen, whose father, a dragonfly aficionado, had recently passed away. The evening he opened the package from me, he phoned Helen, who lives in Humarock, Massachusetts (almost to Cape Cod). He dropped everything and drove to Humarock to deliver the treasure in the middle of the night. I received a heartfelt telephone thank you from Helen.

Aama and Pramod arrived in the US, but Aama's husband died and she had to return to Nepal.

The political and economic situation stabilized and the Maoist activity subsided. Larry feels confident taking another group to Nepal in July 2006.

I wonder whether Baby Olivia ever got her visa.

I am re-evaluating my newspaper reporter status and have turned down several assignments. I have a quote on my refrigerator that I look at each morning. It reads: "Journalism is literature in a hurry." I can't decide whether that's a good thing or a bad thing, or how it applies to me.

I haven't yet decided what I am going to do with my new expertise. I have been more open about what I do and I try to listen to that still, small voice that keeps me walking in both ordinary and non-ordinary reality.

Two southern Maine newspapers interviewed me and my alma maters asked for summaries of my trip. Hiram College in Ohio received a descriptive piece from four of my classmates who had completed a kayaking expedition in Laos about the same time I was in Nepal. Paul Ward, Pete Mitchell, Bob Benedict and Roger Cooper had said to one another exactly what Art had said to me: "If not now, when?"

# BOOK LIST

*As a former librarian, and the daughter of a world-class reader, I am always noticing what others are reading. During our trip I made marginal notes of books people talked about, referred to, or were reading. Aside from some pulp fiction distractions, I have listed here the marginal references I made during our Nepali adventure.*

**Andrews, Lynn V. "Medicine Woman".** An autobiographical account of a woman's search for identity in a Native American culture. What begins as a search for a Native American marriage basket becomes Lynn Andrews' often terrifying journey into the wilderness of Manitoba, where inexplicable events and dangerous encounters serve as testing grounds for her spiritual journey. HarperSanFrancisco (1981).

**Arrien, Angeles "The Four Fold Way: Walking the Paths of the Warrior, Teacher, Healer and Visionary."** An account of spiritual approaches in various cultures and an interpretation of shamanic traditions. HarperSanFrancisco (1993).

**Cowan, Thomas Dale "Shamanism as a Spiritual Practice for Daily Life".** This book shows how to develop a personal spiritual practice by blending elements of shamanism with inherited traditions and current religious commitments. Genealogical Services (1996).

**Dowman, Keith; and Kevin Bubriski, photographer "Power Places of Kathmandu: Hindu and Buddhist Holy Sites in the Sacred Valley of Nepal".** Award-winning photographer Kevin Bubriski captures in stunning detail the sacred places of Nepal's Kathmandu Valley. Noted scholar Keith Dowman provides history and commentary on the significance of the sites. Inner Traditions (1995).

**Garimar, Doris Pilkington "Rabbit-Proof Fence: The True Story of One of the Greatest Escapes of All Time".** In the small Australian village of Jigalong, three half-caste children, sisters Molly (14) and Daisy (8), and their cousin, 10-

year old Gracie, are taken from their mothers to live in the orphanage at Moore River, more than 1200 miles away from their home. There, they will learn the path of "duty, service, and responsibility" that every good Christian woman should adhere to. Except that Molly, Daisy, and Gracie are not like the other girls at Moore River, and, when an opportunity presents itself, they escape. Pursued by an Aborigine tracker, Moodoo, and facing a seemingly impossible trek, they press on, finding the rabbit-proof fence that stretches north to south across nearly the entire Australian continent and follow it as a means to return to Jigalong. Phillip Noyce's film *Rabbit-Proof Fence* is based on the book. Miramax Books (2002).

**Harner, Michael "The Way of the Shaman".** A good basic book on shamanic practice. HarperSanFrancisco 10th Anniversary edition (1990).

**Ingerman, Sandra "Soul Retrieval: Mending the Fragmented Self Through Shamanic Practice".** If the soul totally vacates the patient, the patient will die. It follows that, if the shaman can retrieve lost soul parts, the individual can be restored to harmony and well-being. HarperSanFrancisco (1991).

**Morgan, Marlo "Mutant Message Down Under: A Woman's Journey into Dreamtime Australia".** Aborigines offer the storyteller a chance to learn firsthand about their culture. Morgan's account of the tribe's customs, healing methods, food-finding tactics, etc. is absorbing. Reed Business Information, Inc. (1994).

**Narby, Jeremy "The Cosmic Serpent, DNA and the Origin of Knowledge"** Research indicates that shamans access an intelligence that has stunning correspondences with molecular biology. There seems to be a capacity to make choices operating inside each cell in our body. Any one cell is listening to hundreds of signals at the same time, and has to integrate them and decide what to do. How this intelligence operates is the question. This author thinks that science of shamans can complement modern science by helping make sense of the data it generates. Shamanism is like a reverse camera relative to modern science. Tarcher; New Ed edition (1999).

**Perkins, John "Confessions of an Economic Hitman: How the US Uses Globalization to Cheat Poor Countries Out of Trillions"** Plume; Reprint edition (2005).

**Roberts, Richard "I Was Much Happier When Everything I Owned Was in the Back Seat of My Volkswagen: A Wake-up Call for the Biggest Generation".** Can Baby Boomers save America? The author thinks it will take a return to the activism of the Sixties. In an unsettling look at current events, he concludes that time is running out. Our money is being confiscated, our freedoms restricted, our movements videotaped, and we're being pumped full of medications and lies 'for our own good'. Baby Boomer Press (2004).

**Robertson, Laurel, Carol Flinders and Brian Ruppenthal "Laurel's Kitchen"** Healthy, tasty vegetarian meals your family will actually eat. If you are looking for a way to incorporate vegetables, grains and legumes into your diet but think there aren't too many options – this is the cookbook you need. Ten Speed Press; Revised edition (1993).

**Thomas, Lesley "Flight of the Goose".** A love story between two people of very different cultures set against the fragile world of the Alaskan Arctic. The author portrays the Inupiaq people in their struggle to survive, as well as their spiritual kinship with their ancient homeland. Far Eastern Press (2005).

**Villoldo, Alberto "Healing States: A Journey Into the World of Spiritual Healing and Shamanism".** An examination of evidence for the mind's ability to heal, taking a step into the world of psychic healing and shamanism. Fireside (1987).

**Watson, Lyall "Heaven's breath: A natural history of the Wind".** An examination of various aspects of wind. William Morrow & Co; 1st U.S. edition (1985).

**Weil, Andrew "Healthy Aging: A Lifelong Guide to Your Physical and Spiritual Well-Being"** One cannot stop the changes of time, but you can modify lifestyle and activity as you age, and it is good to know that help is available to maintain the efficiency of your healing system. Knopf (2005).

**Wright, Machaell Small "MAP The Co-Creative White Brotherhood Medical Assistance Program".** MAP is a medical program in which you work with energy beings and nature intelligences. MAP is a physical program that works on your well-being from the physical, emotional, mental, and spiritual perspective. It works on strains, pressures, pain, and conflict felt at all these levels simultaneously. Perelandra Ltd. (1974).

# Tibetan Shamanism Workshop Series
## Led by Dr. Larry G. Peters, PhD

Each of the four workshops in the series is devoted to sharing shamanic healing and ritual techniques practiced by Tibetan Bön shamans in the Nepali Himalayas, where shamanism is a living healing system. Dr. Larry Peters PhD is a licensed psychotherapist, author, professor, and an initiated shaman in this tradition.

Participants should be familiar with shamanic journeying and power animals. You should bring something to sit on, a drum or rattle, eyeshade or bandana, something personal for the group altar, and a sacred intention for the weekend workshop. Workshops need not be taken in order as each is complete in itself and has its own ritual focus.

**Tibetan Shamanism 1:**
**Mandala of Shapes, Lights, Elements & Directions**

A key pilgrimage site for Tibetans is the sacred reliquary structure known as "stupa." As a symbolic form the stupa embodies the essential elements and goals of shamanic, as well as Tibetan Buddhist, practice. Each of its five levels represents a color, shape, element, and direction, as well as the chakra energy and state of consciousness gifted by the Buddha who resides there. These are the five Meditation Buddhas. The purpose of this workshop is to experience, in journey, meditation, and masked dance, the dynamic energies of the spirit elements, directions, and lights, for personal growth, inspiration, and realization. The workshop has an initiatory structure and purpose, culminating in a "nature journey" to enlist the aid of the elemental spirits for healing of the community, the planet and all beings.

**Tibetan Shamanism 2:**
**Techniques of Healing with Spiritual Extraction**

Spiritual extraction techniques can be used to heal individual patients as well as for community cleansing. This workshop focuses on healing techniques practiced by the Tibetan Bön shamans. These skills are taught through guided journeys and shamanic practices embodying spirit in dance for the healing of self and others.

### Tibetan Shamanism 3:
### Soul Retrieval and Psychopomp Process

Soul retrieval is a multi-faceted tradition involving ritual skills as well as the journeywork of the shamanic practitioner. Soul retrieval is more often than not combined with other healing processes like extraction, divination, spirit invocation, and psychopomp work. When these multiple processes are involved, the ritual as a whole is often known as karga puja (spirit weapon ceremony). In this workshop, the group first learns and then performs the karga puja ritual.

### Tibetan Shamanism 4:
### Chöd, Community Cleansing, and the Cosmos

This workshop includes an introduction to techniques like pho-wa (transference of consciousness) and chöd (the sacrifice of hindrances to spiritual awakening) and is both learned and enacted, conferring shamanic abilities for soul retrieval, journey work with the dead and dying, and healing of self, others, the community, and the planet. The format of this workshop is the guru puja initiation.

**PILGRIMAGES TO NEPAL**

Dr. Peters also takes groups like ours to Nepal on a regular basis. The sacred journey to Nepal allows for deep immersion into the culture, spirituality, and healing practices of Tibetan, Tamang, and other tribal shamans. Information on these pilgrimages are on Peters' website. If you decide to partake of this adventure, please tell him Sue Melanson sent you!

Contact:
Dr. Larry G. Peters, Ph. D.
1212 Old Topanga Canyon Road
Topanga, CA 90290
(310) 455-2713
www.TibetanShaman.com
lpshaman@aol.com

# ABOUT THE AUTHOR

*Sue Melanson 2006*

Susan Chapman Melanson began her literary training in Miss Teed's English class at Wellesley High School in Massachusetts. She attended Colby Junior College in New Hampshire (now called Colby-Sawyer College) and Hiram College in Ohio. She is also an honorary member of the Northfield School Class of 1964. Her roots are in Wellesley and Reading, Massachusetts but she moved to Oak Hill Farm in South Hiram, Maine in 1995 with her husband, Captain Arthur Melanson. Sue Melanson is now an herbalist, shamanic practitioner, author and a reporter for the *Sacopee Valley Citizen*. Together the Melansons operate High Acres Maple Syrup and The Cottages at Oak Hill Farm.

Contact:
Susan Chapman Melanson
Oak Hill Farm
14 Husky Haven
South Hiram, Maine 04041
(207) 625-7151
melanson@oakhillfarm.com
www.oakhillfarm.com

*Also by this author:*

**"Wentworth-By-The-Sea, 1969 - A Novel"**
**By Susan Chapman Melanson**

A time capsule about life in a special place in a special time. The first person story is told from the perspective of a waitress in one of the last of the grand resort hotels on the seacoast of New Hampshire. The semi-historic tale includes a fascinating cast of characters, detailed descriptions of the inner workings of the dining room and kitchen, local legends, pop music references and comments on the times. 1969 was the year the first man walked on the moon, the year Teddy Kennedy's car plunged off the bridge at Chappaquidick, the year Prince Charles was appointed Duke of Wales and was feted at Wentworth-By-The-Sea in a Grand Ball, and the year of Woodstock. It was also the end of an era for the elite resort life that Wentworth-By-The-Sea represented. (Xlibris 2000)

Available through
www.xlibris.com
1-888-795-4274

*Also by this author:*

**"Confessions of The Classmate Who Never Was, Northfield School for Girls Class of 1964"
By Susan Chapman Melanson**

As a sixteen year old, the author spent a summer working at the Northfield Conferences, which were held on the campus of Northfield School for Girls in the rolling hills of western Massachusetts right where Vermont, New Hampshire and Massachusetts intersect. She fell in love with the place, the people and the enchanting Chateau that overlooked the Connecticut River. Unable to persuade her parents to send her to the boarding school, she settled for dreaming about the place, and one summer she invented a temporary persona for herself in which she was an alumna of Northfield. As an adult she began giving annually to the alumnae fund and a confused secretary from the alumnae office called her asking what class she had been a member of. Why, 1964, of course! After that she was regularly solicited for alumnae giving, and invited to reunions. In 2004 she returned to Northfield for "her" 40th Reunion. This is that story, including a substantial section on the history of the Northfield Chateau, complete with pictures and floor plans. (Lulu 2006)

Available through
www.lulu.com

"If not now, when?"